Shared Visions

Thoughts and Experiences in Social Arts Practice

Merrill • Powers • Rehagen

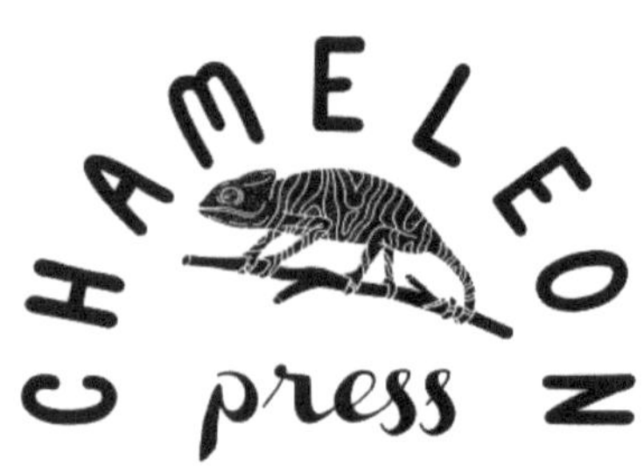

Chameleon Press
Kansas City, MO
www.chameleonartskc.org

First Edition, 2014
Second Edition, 2018

ISBN: 9780999022214
Library of Congress Control Number: 2018932273

Cover: Haley Hatch and Chameleon Arts, *Ghost Drawing*, Emmanuel's Community Center, Kansas City, Missouri, 2013.

All images in book courtesy of Chameleon photo archives, unless otherwise noted.

Acknowledgments

Chameleon Arts would like to thank all of our dedicated artists, the poets who have spoken for justice, the young people we have served with arts programming, and the many schools and social agencies with whom we have worked. We had no idea 24 years ago that the agency would have helped so many people of varied circumstances and communities. We are humbled by our past history and lifted up by the opportunities of the present and future.

None of this work would have been possible without the help of many foundations and organizations who understand the importance of art in creating positive social change. We wish to thank these supporters: The National Endowment for the Arts, the Missouri Arts Council, the ArtsKC Regional Arts Council, the R.A Long Foundation, Francis Family Foundation, Lawrence A. and Joan S. Weiner, Muriel McBrien Kaufman, H&R Block Foundations, and our many private donors.

We express further thanks to Samantha Slupski, Caitlin Daily, Poetic Underground, Uptown Arts Bar, Al Pitzner, Walter L. Cofer, Nicola Heskett, Dr. Luz and Antony Racela, Staci Pratt, Adelia Ganson, Jacqueline Chanda, Amanda Rehagen, Majikah Perfumery, Ed Hogan, Dorothy Dunn, Mel Chin, Eric Fischl, Lynn Kauffman, Todd Weiner Gallery and Rita Blitt.

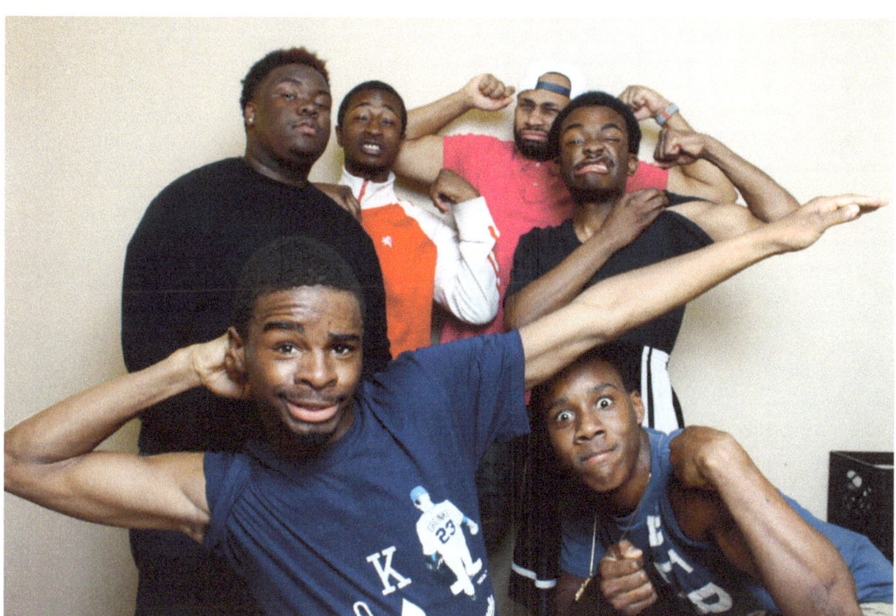

Emmanuel's Community Center, 35th and Prospect, Kansas City, MO, 2014.

Table of Contents

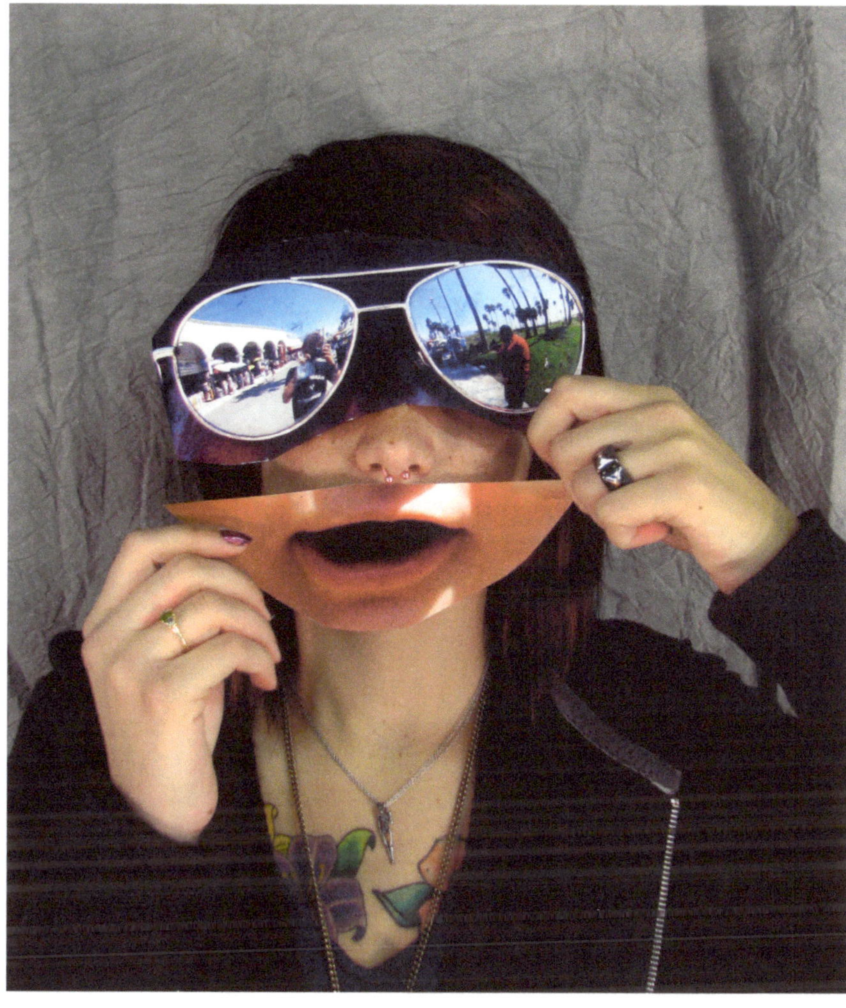

Introduction

The creation of art takes fragments of an existence and pulls them into a whole. Art is fun. Building and making things is a joy, whether those things are musical compositions, visual art works, sculptures, poems, conceptual ideas or something else. Art isn't neatly defined or categorized.

Art is a reason to go to bed early and stay up late. It is a way to help kids in the inner city, a way to keep track of life, a way to keep time. Art helps to teach. It is a connector, a catalyst, a communicator. Art can be anything. Art can be what we say it is or serve a purpose we need at the time. It is a technical process or the personification of an abstract thought. It is for the greater good in all of us.

Sometime in the summer of 1968, in Billings, Montana, an easel saved me from seemingly certain doom as a non-conformist child in a conservative family. I was six. I had been sitting on the wooden deck in my parent's backyard drawing on a pad with a pencil and ruining my knees, according to my mother.

My neighbor had seen my efforts and sensed my need to make art and dropped off an easel for me. She was from somewhere on the East Coast and her name was Sarah Helen.

At my art lessons at the local center, I learned about famous artists. Most had lived in Europe, far away from my home, although some of them were still alive and living in New York. Most had been dead for a long time and nearly all of them were men. As I continued to study art history, I learned about a few women artists. They had far fewer museum and gallery shows than their male counterparts and were nearly non-existent in the art history texts I was assigned in school. About careers as an artist for women, the early careers of the Guerilla Girls and others reminded us of the disproportionate role of white men of European descent.

The traditional art historical canon has diminished in influence, but many students of art are still exposed to this reference point for artistic progress and validity. In 1971, Linda Nochlin asked the question: "Why are there no great women artists?" in an essay of the same name.[1] Nochlin asserted that from a historical standpoint it was extraordinarily difficult for even immensely talented and accomplished women to achieve true success in a male-dominated pursuit. Feminist artists answered the question with a tidal wave of response. They confronted their most visceral issues, from violence to gay rights, women's concerns and issues of the oppressed. Suzanne Lacy, Judy Chicago, Barbara Kruger and the Guerrilla Girls are a small part of the army of women artists who put feminist art on the map through their hauntingly relevant work. Social critic and feminist champion Lucy Lippard helped to further communicate a demand for change in the established methods of thinking about art and the views of the artists.[2] There have always been artists within all demographic groups. Their work may not have been written about or recorded, but the need to create art has always existed.

Feminist artists did a lot of heavy lifting to advance the cause for the "other." Their work asked not only "who is an artist?" but as importantly, confronted the idea that art can be created anywhere, and that non-traditional art could hold as much importance as museum art. Perhaps more importantly, art found a place in the social fabric of communities.

The idea that all great artists are disproportionately male is still assumed in many classrooms today. The majority of the art made by people not white and male was ignored until the 1970s, when creative pressures bubbled forth and permanently changed the demographic of who could make art. The traditional hierarchy of museum exhibition as a career was matched by a corresponding path of collective and social engagement. With a parallel history established, feminist, LGBT, at-risk and other minority groups changed the face of art history as it moved forward.

Through the women's movement, a new vantage point emerged. The outlook of "the other," meaning anyone not male and white, was being recorded and considered. The first wave of feminist art served as a social catalyst, igniting an alternative and never before exposed dialogue on the human condition. These artists were not afraid to deal with issues such as rape, abuse and failed societal remedies.

M. Anna Fariello states in her essay *Making and Naming: The Lexicon of Studio Craft* that craft is "bound to the hand, to the process of working, of making." Social practice art can be viewed in a similar fashion, as it is bound to the participants. It cannot exist without a symbiotic partner. Only through actuality is the work capable of functioning, of making a difference for the people it serves.[3]

Shared Visions lays out a theoretical and conceptual framework for socially interactive arts actions informed by the writing and work of many: Lucy Lippard, Joseph Beuys, Nicolas Bourriaud, Beth Krensky and Seana Lowe Steffan, Suzanne

Lacy, Mary Jane Jacob, Tim Rollins, Suzi Gablik, John Dewey and others. Our hope is that the ideas pulled together here will provide a structure to help initiate and sustain social practice programs nationally in schools, colleges and universities.

The ability to think creatively is touted by business, politics and most forms of media. How do we learn to think creatively? How do you help someone learn life skills?

These issues clearly raise the question of art's value in society: If artists have success in honing their creative abilities through the study of artistic practice, can the general public benefit from similar studies? How can people who have little access to cultural events, or education in their appreciation, begin to become familiar with these concepts?

Chameleon Arts and Youth Development (CAYD) has helped youth in Kansas City's urban core struggle with these questions for many years. We have seen former participants succeed through college graduation and move into careers. Some have started families, while others are attending community colleges.

For many children living in downtown Kansas City considered beyond risk, money and confidence are seldom available. Funds are often in short supply and life situations are complicated by poverty, in conjunction with drug and gang culture. In neighborhoods where guns and drugs destroy safety and security, warm fuzzy feelings about the future are few and far between. *Shared Visions* outlines exercises to build confidence and self-esteem that CAYD has successfully used for over 20 years. Not only were beyond-risk children served but additional participants include: college students, K-12 teachers and administrators, homeless advocates and social workers. Through CAYD arts actions, exhibitions and projects, thousands of children and everyday folks have been informed and deeply affected. These programs and their supporting workshops have also been facilitated all over the United States, as well as China, Guatemala, Ireland, Cuba and Poland.

Many of the clients participating in social practice art actions are just learning how to apply creativity to their life. Many have seldom thought of capturing their lives or feelings through writing or artwork. The *Portrait of Self* (POS) archiving process provides individuals with the means to keep a history of their experiences through artistic expression. A journal that portrays their life experience and records their personality. Their joys, sorrows and concerns are all reflected. Some reflect the very harsh realities of their own lives. The POS process allows them a new way to evaluate and consider their lives and choices often leading to new positive behavior patterns.

Creative thinking can become embedded into the collective personality of a society. Once people become exposed to alternative methods of thinking, these tools for life spread themselves through groups of people. Instead of roaming the streets wherever, doing whatever, troubled teens can build skills to help them make positive choices every day. They can take the creative knowledge and experience with them and help to disseminate it to others.

In 1995, critic and author Suzi Gablik wrote about what she saw as a new concept in art. *The Re-Enchantment of Art* claims the work is significantly different than what many saw as art, in general. At the time, she was criticized because some of the work in the book utilized social and environmental concerns as a media, which was looked upon with suspicion and doubt.[4]

Major strides have been made in college programs over the past several years. Many times, social practice curriculum has evolved from printmaking, which is a primarily democratic media, similar to social arts. Social arts are a form of work that everyone can participate in and where everyone can create. There is no longer the question of what art can be, or who can be considered an artist. The application of creative thinking makes it possible to affect people from a potent place where they live, where the work becomes relevant to them. In an age where images are everywhere and are used continually in advertising and popular culture, it is not surprising that the age of image-based art is not as important as it once was. Although exhibiting work maintains importance for reflection, the validation of the art is no longer dependent on a gallery wall. It has become the people it serves.

Artist Rirkrit Tiravanija has said: "It is not what you see that is important, but what takes place between people." The majority of Tiravanija's work has been concerned with social interactions, as opposed to the creation of a formal work of art exhibited on a wall space. His concentration on and commitment to the creation of new kinds of spaces is filled with the possibility of interaction.[5] He drew the attention of Nicolas Bourriaud when he set the stage for people to create their own meal in the home of a collector. This work has been duplicated all over the world, in museums and other galleries, where people have been invited to cook and eat Thai food at no charge.

Tiravanija has created an 84' print, *Untitled, 2008-2011*, using many traditional media: inkjet printing, silkscreen, lithography and chine collé, in a shift from conceptualism to object making. The piece created was so large it sometimes required the help of up to five assistants, bringing it back into the realm of collaboration.[6]

Even though relational aesthetics and project art have both played key roles in the arts over the past few decades, they are still de-emphasized in arts education in many areas. Art critics have become accustomed to socially based media and have seen it as a form of establishment art for some time[7], but many students of the arts still get limited exposure to these well-established concepts. The same can be said of relational antagonism, which presents an opposing view to relational aesthetics and its theory. This disconnect appears to be built-in to an institutionally based learning structure. The terms used to describe socially interactive art are used as synonyms by some, and are seen with specific delineation by others. In this publication, the use of these terms is context specific.

Digital and social media as art materials have the potential to take creativity nearly anywhere, as they are truly changing the world. Twitter was a major influence in political movements, like the Arab Spring and Occupy. Facebook, Pinterest and Tumblr have all become valuable online marketing and sales tools for artists. Crowdfunding platforms like Kickstarter and Indiegogo provide alternative methods of exposure and financing. Artists frequently create websites as art projects, often allowing other online users to contribute if they choose.

Beck released the album *Song Reader*, in the form of sheet music only. It consists of 20 songs that were never released or recorded that are designed to be played by the audience. Beck has found a way to disappear into the background by allowing the audience to directly participate in the music. Like social practice artists, he has facilitated the germination of creativity. He has recently said that he wanted for the audience to "not just re-mix the songs, but play them like a video game."[8]

Artists can be found everywhere in everyday life. Someone with a garden in their front yard uses flowers as a medium for artistic expression. A teacher creates a lesson that engages and empowers students to act on their ideas and passions. Neighborhood groups gather for social events that become works of art on multiple levels. These artists are sometimes clandestine that recognizing their work immediately can be difficult. Some of them have no interest in drawing, painting or taking pictures. Instead, the media they use is a combination of social justice and empowerment. To reach beyond the stereotypical "art for the people" requires not only the knowledge that art can help people, but that it is essential for all of us in the future.

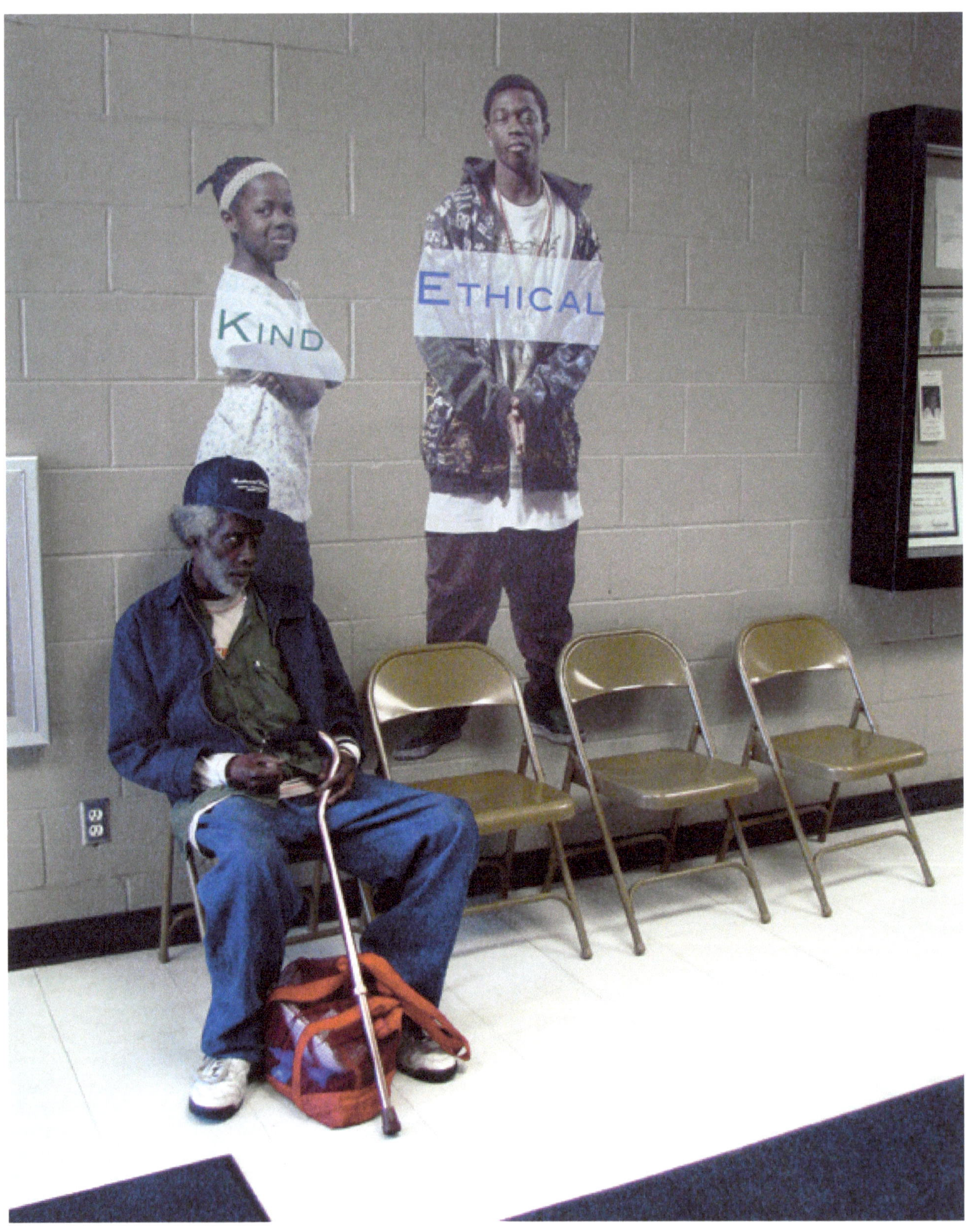

KIND
ETHICAL

Opposite page:
Faces of the Homeless, installation at the Willa Gill Resource
Center, Kansas City, Kansas, 2011.

Chapter 1:
Lay of the Land

The artist who is entering into a community must be aware of the cultural and historical landscape in which they will work. If the aim of the community arts action is moving toward empowerment, social justice and equality, a basic understanding of political and economic realities is of significant value. These concerns are multiplied when the artist is different from the community by race, faith, class or other demographic measure.

This realization moves the artist beyond creative art theories that outline or support community art and social practice. Whether they realize it or not, artists working with marginalized communities must understand and confront deep social, political, and economic issues that cannot be skipped over and must be addressed directly. These issues are complex and of immense importance to sustaining a community (or society) and the role of the artist in mediating and confronting these issue should not be underestimated.

Here we will only open the doors to several of these issues. In this text we cannot go into to the depth of investigation needed to understand their complexity. We can at this stage point them out and be a map to help show the way toward individual investigation by the reader.

Race and Culture

The community artist often will not be of the same race, culture, faith, background and economic class as the community they are engaging. It is important that the person can go beyond sensitivity and more deeply understand the viewpoint of the folks they are working with. Race is a real issue and a difficult maze to navigate for many, especially white folks.

When George Zimmerman shot and killed African-American teen Trayvon Martin, most folks of color felt that if he had been a white kid in a hoodie Zimmerman would not have pulled the trigger. Many felt he would not have even followed the young man.

After the verdict, an all-white jury expressed that the case was not about race, but about the "stand your ground" gun law in Florida, and that Zimmerman was simply defending himself. He was out walking around with a gun, following Martin, which led to the fight that precipitated the shooting. Folks of color knew better.

Around the age of thirteen, African-American men are pulled aside by others and told to be conscious of where they are, where they are walking and who is in front of and behind them. They are reminded that racial tension is only one complaint or sidelong glance away. It is through this lens that they view the world.

It is now widely accepted that the war on drugs is actually a war on the poor and/or brown people, resulting in mass incarceration[1] facilitated by a for-profit prison system.[2] In her book *The New Jim Crow*, professor, attorney and activist Michelle Alexander articulates techniques used by law enforcement and reinforced by courts over recent decades, effectively enforcing a permanent lower caste system.[3] Alexander contends that the label of "felon" follows people who have been released from prison, making it nearly impossible for them to get any type of legal job.[4] Many times, the terms of their parole depend on them paying fines and court costs and sometimes even the entire cost of their incarceration. Their wages can be garnished up to 100% to repay these fees, nearly ensuring financial collapse.[5]

White folks, even with the best of intentions, will not always see race as a major issue contributing to the decisions that precede fairness, economic opportunity, equality and social justice. White folks often do not see what they cannot experience. Many of our core social and economic problems are rooted in class: fair access to health care, the minimum wage, affirmative action, quality education or the means to start a business are all class issues.

Spanish artist Sierra has stated: "I can't change anything. There is no possibility that we can change anything with our work."[6] Sierra, noted as a relational antagonist, is interested in the participation of people in making arts projects, but stops just shy of where things get interesting, as he advocates an abbreviated response to potential and possibility. Arts projects can and do benefit thousands of our nation's neediest children.[7]

In an email to art historian, teacher and theorist Claire Bishop, artist Thomas Hirschorn said:

> *"I want to work out an alternative to this lazy, lousy, 'democratic' and demagogic term 'Participation'. I am not for 'Participative-art', it's so stupid because every old painting makes you more 'participating' than today's 'Participative-art', because first of all real participation is the participation of thinking! Participation is only another word for 'Consumption'!*[8]

Bishop's critique of socially engaged art contends that it leaves little to critical reflection, and less to visual satisfaction, leaving a questionable outcome.[9] She states that after her lectures, people sometimes ask her about outcomes: "Even if one person is saved, does that make an event worthwhile?" they ask. Bishop's interpretation of a visually bereft socially engaged art movement, overshadowed by professionally produced visually compelling work, constitute an absence of appreciation for much of the reason behind the work. Does assuming that art has a limited function in society burden it unnecessarily?

For facilitators working with at-risk teenagers in detention or community centers, where "participative-art" is utilized as a means to reduce violence for inner city kids with behavioral issues, the reasoning goes in the opposite direction. About arts programs involving incarcerated and homeless kids, Chameleon Arts and Youth Development's Executive Director Hugh Merrill says:

> *"We have had great success in helping the kids achieve calmer moods. The program has also helped their concentration and self-esteem issues. These kids come from some rough backgrounds, many of their parents are or have been in jail or prison, and many of their friends and family are addicted to drugs. Since they don't have positive role models, it is difficult for them to visualize a different life for themselves. Our projects help them to think outside this world and to begin the precursors of societal learning. Our programs increase both their understanding of concepts and their grades and evaluations at school."*[10]

There is a fundamental problem with socially engaged art. Collectors aren't usually interested. Some generous donors and foundations are involved in funding the work, if it has been exhibited and can demonstrate documented positive outcomes. Some types of participatory public art projects have done better in the traditional art market, but community based work is not usually an economic engine.

Chameleon Arts and Youth Development works with children in Kansas City's urban core, many of whom are considered beyond-risk.[11] These children represent collateral damage in a heavily armed society. Many have family members who have been the victims of gun violence and some have been injured themselves. Specific programs have been developed by Chameleon artists to help these children begin the healing process. The programs have received high marks from social workers and educators that work at schools or community centers. Chameleon has proven that arts programs help to teach life-skills and raise self-esteem in even these neighborhoods. Some participants have gone to school at community colleges or universities, and a few have had the opportunity to attend elite schools like Duke University or the Kansas City Art Institute.

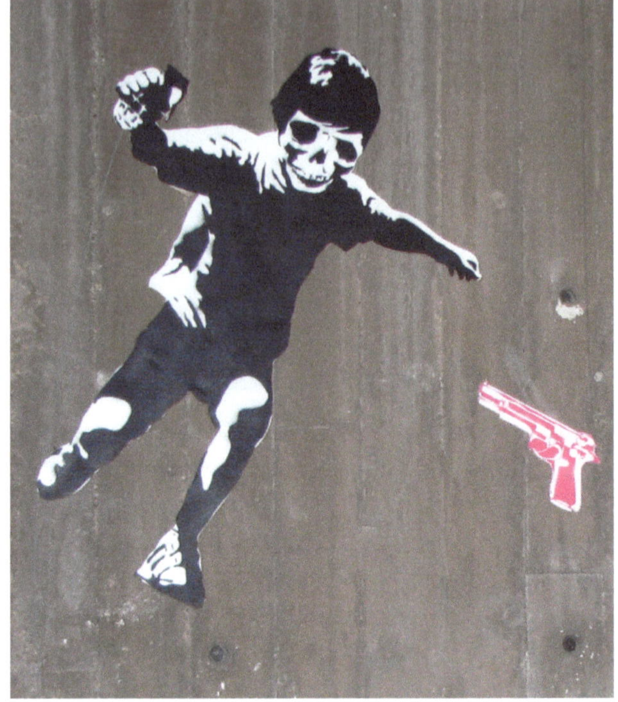

Children of the Gun

It's always the kids who pay the price.
– Myra Morgan[12]

Kansas City's ZIP code 64130 is a community 8 square miles in size that is so immersed in gun violence that it is called the murder factory.[13] It is within a few blocks of Chameleon Art's offices. In 2009, Kansas City Star journalist Tony Rizzo sent questionnaires to the 101 people from 64130 incarcerated for involuntary manslaughter, or murder in the state of Missouri. Also included were responses from 270 other people from around the state convicted of the same crimes. Here is a sampling of their responses:

- 2/3 possessed firearms as teenagers.
- Many stated they had observed few examples of legitimate success.
- They said the area itself offered few alternatives.
- A cultural mentality requiring street violence as a knee-jerk response.
- Easy access to drugs and guns.[14]

While not as dangerous as 64130, other areas of downtown Kansas City have high arrest and incarceration rates disproportionately affecting the African-American community. Nearly every day there is a local news story of a shooting. Many times young children, including infants, are among the victims.

By ensuring a free flow of firearms through the US marketplace, another assurance is made: all citizens do not have the right to a safe world. The right to not be shot at does not exist in the US. In the shadow of 64130, kids need positive interactions and access to cultural activities. Many times, the positive results can be calculated and documented.[15]

We must remember that to enter the discussion for economic and social equity, we pass through the gateway of race, and are forced to acknowledge what the differences in class really mean. People of color make up 60% of the prison population.[16] People who exit the prison system with a felony on their record are not ever allowed to vote in many states. If their families or friends live in public housing, they risk being evicted by allowing them to visit.[17]

Racial discrimination is not an abstract concept, it is an underlying reality that can only be overcome by acknowledging its presence. The Civil Rights movement is not a period in history, but is instead an ongoing struggle. As long as there is class struggle, the politics of division, blame and hatred will attempt to drive a wedge between the haves and the have-nots. In short: the fight for equality lasts forever.

The Power of Capitalism

We live in a corporate capitalist economy system, where those in power have access to the political system to have regulations and laws passed to benefit their ability to increase profits and increase their ability to control and benefit from the system. So we see that corporations are people, and that elections are being bought by the rich and powerful. A system has been created that is dependent on the weakest in society remaining ignorant in an attempt to deny them their right to vote. This is a difficult reality to change.

A single community arts project of course will not change this, but recognition of the power imbalance will help to direct our voices and efforts to challenge the inequity of the system. Fighting intelligently and with commitment through artistic creative action is a meaningful and significant response.

Placemaking and Gentrification

Placemaking is about buildings and spaces first and the people that use, live or enter into the spaces are secondary concerns.[18]

Placemaking uses multi-faceted approaches to planning, design and management of public spaces, most often leading to gentrification, the taking over of a community by and for outsiders based on their potential wealth. The folks who lived in the area are forced out due to increased rents, property taxes and the erosion of their community culture. Race and class are often a major factor with people of color and modest income becoming displaced and replaced by a white urban professional demographic. At its worst, this process leads to exclusion and polarization of the original community.

Artists are often among the first to move in and re-develop marginal urban neighborhoods. In the first stage of development, the local community's assets, inspiration, and potential are included in the revitalization which comes from the grass roots up. This philosophy is known as placemaking, which moves on to gentrification. This is a tried and true method of generating interest in marginal neighborhoods by developers. As the area exhibits more economic opportunity, the local community is forced out and developers and politicians take over and accelerate the process of gentrification. The goal of revitalizing the community by creating spaces that promote health, happiness, and well-being are often lost in the developer's search for profits.

A well-known business model for real-estate agents, this has happened from Brooklyn Heights, New York, to Watergate and Foggy Bottom in Washington, D.C., and most large American cities.

A journal on the subject *Places: Forum of Design for the Public Realm*, is about the design of places, the experiences they make possible and the consequences they have in our lives.

Neoliberal capitalism has reinforced a market-based response to most real estate in cities all over the globe. The wide acceptance of the role of artists in placemaking as a precursor to gentrification illuminates this contemporary reality of adopting, renting, or purchasing work, studio or gallery spaces. Where many of these spaces can bring success for artists and/or gallerists, there remains a significant number of creative people whose efforts turn into profit for real estate companies, as opposed to providing a long term solution to needed retail or work space.

In the early 1990s, a group of artists in Kansas City, Missouri, answered a series of newspaper ads for "artist space." These ads featured wording like "full design freedom," and "unlimited design possibilities." When the group looked at the properties, they found a number of problems, including: no access to plumbing, no heat or missing windows or no access to electricity. One of the leasing managers was open to artists providing their own bathrooms, but it was later revealed that no water lines were functional in the space. Other spaces were more reasonably priced, but many still did not have on-site bathrooms, requiring a three block bolt to the nearest sympathetic retailer.

In the early 2000s, a gallery in a Midwestern city moved to a more popular part of town, in the hope of generating more foot traffic and sales. The gallery owner expressed some dissatisfaction in the functionality of the space. The owner/developer offered to renovate the space specifically for them at a substantially increased cost. The gallery owner agreed, focusing on a desire to build up a success story and participate in a thriving artistic community.

Within 2 years, the gallerists ran out of money to pay the rent, but the building owner had an improved space to rent to others chasing their own dreams. Since the developer contracted the work himself, he didn't have to worry about outstanding unpaid debt to someone else.

The entire arrangement was designed to sell the gallery owners the idea of a successful personal/professional labor of love and, as importantly, to upsell them an expensive construction loan. Financial products, such as payday loans or car title loans, are often marketed to people with little or no understanding of the industry that offers them, or why they are being sold to begin with. This is evidenced by a high default rate on repayment of these loan products. Many times people who use these services are desperate financially or are reacting emotionally to the prospect of receiving money. These same techniques are successfully applied by developers and real estate companies to the lease, sales or rehabilitation of spaces that are marketed to artists.

A solid deal for the developer turned out to be a sour deal for the gallery tenant, who overestimated the ability of the business to pay an increased rent on the property. It was not a solid enough idea to generate the amount of capital needed for a commercially successful venue. A challenging retail climate and a soft economy contributed to the failure of the idea.

Fortunately for developers, there is a never ending number of artists, performers, gallerists and other creative types willing to take a financial risk following their dreams, which ultimately improves the property, and corporate profits and margins. While owning your own business can give unlimited income and possibilities, it is not always so. Overextension on retail, theme park or studio space is one of the main reasons newly minted artists or creative businesses fail. The presumed displacement of artists, gallerists or other exhibition spaces is an accepted and desired role of the market run economy involving the spaces of neoliberalism.[19]

What is the role of community engaged art in social conscience?

In 1968, Institutional Act No. 5, also known as A1-5, was passed in Brazil. It suspended political and civil rights. This change resulted in self-censorship on the part of artists, but it also caused artists to communicate through the passage of messages, almost as a form of alternative language.[20]

Chinese artist Ai Weiwei has been jailed, his money and studio seized, by Chinese authorities because of the strong opinions voiced in his work. He states that almost all of the questions asked by interrogators had to do with his political activism.[21] The Gao Brothers, also from China, send out tweets letting people know where their openings are, to avoid police contact.[22] It is easy to proclaim that art has no impact on political events, as it cannot stop a war or free people who are oppressed, yet it is often the free thinkers: artists, musicians and poets that are the first to be silenced when an oppressive regime takes power.

Walter Gropius' Bauhaus represents an extreme example of the progression of a regime upon artistic vision. Only in existence from

1919 to 1933, in three German cities, Bauhaus was founded upon a belief in the power of involvement and a merging of artistic discipline with workers, while producing a wide array of consumer products. Forced out by the Nazis, the artists that taught at the Bauhaus moved to elite schools in the United States. Some even formed their own institutions.[23]

Could the Bauhaus have prevented the coming Holocaust? No. But neither could political action or even military action. Syria is a case where the institutional and governmental powers cannot bring an end to a bloody conflict. Why burden art with the assumption that it is useless in confronting serious and intractable human and political problems when these centers of power are impotent?

The song *We Shall Overcome* provided a weapon and ethos for the civil rights movement. George Grosz's *Ecce Homo* drawings expose a degrading society on the verge of Nazism. Grosz's drawings did not prevent Hitler from coming to power but did provide a form of resistance, by establishing a point of view that passionately contrasted the prevailing wave of acceptance and support for Nazism. Those who make art or facilitate arts actions that engage community and are aimed at social change and justice should not so easily be dismissed but critics that hide behind the convenience that art cannot change society. In reality, art is like water dripping continuously on a rock, altering its form significantly. Art does change our society and view of the world we live in, and that is more than enough.

Looking Forward

The future will not look like today. There are vast pressures across the globe to evolve and change the present economic system. More than 3 billion new people will move into urban areas by 2050. There are no real plans for this influx of folks, so the growth of cities will not have a master plan, but will be made possible by community development. The map we see today will not be the same by 2050, new countries and areas now seeking independence will shape a reversal of the age of vast national states, such as the past USSR. The world map will continue to break into smaller and smaller regions. The banking system, based on speculation and a constant bubble economy, will be challenged and changed. There will be winners and losers. The environment, due to global warming, will alter coast lines and climatic conditions leading to unintended consequences.

It is very likely the art that is now held as important, collected by the ultra-rich and nurtured within in a realm of sarcasm and irony, will be a footnote in culture as new artists engage environmental and human issues. The novelty of the new has faded, and the era of art "isms" (Surrealism, Abstract Expressionism, etc.) has long since passed.

Art schools are trying to understand this evolution by starting social practice programs. This change in direction is not yet fully realized. We will see artists continue to be an elite class of makers of culture for the benefit and entertainment of the ultra wealthy well into the future.

Change comes slowly, but that change is well under way, and the momentum is on the side of the humanitarian artist working with and for people, for all.

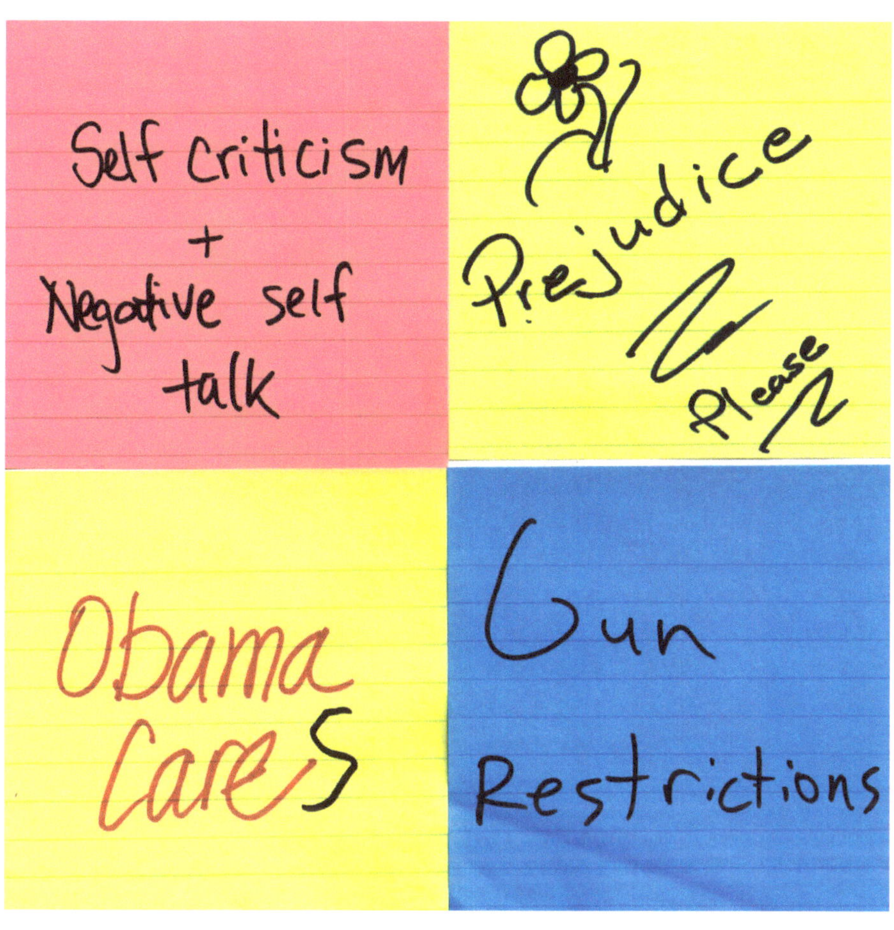

Liberty: Post-It note responses, at *ArtWorkers: Creativity and America*, at the George A. Spiva Art Center Joplin, Missouri, 2013.

Chapter 2:
Thoughts and Experiences in Social Arts Practice

Since the late 1980s, fine art, printmaking and community arts professor Hugh Merrill has worked with children in Kansas City's urban core. Through his personal and professional explorations, he developed this definition:

"Community art is a process and a tool. This process has long-lasting effects, providing methods for evolving personal, political and social changes."[1]

Community art has traditionally attracted artists who have a passion for social justice and change, and who are deeply rooted in the need to make art function in society. They frequently collaborate with people who are disadvantaged or whose cultures are ignored by the mainstream. They see art as an active force in society, not something defined by the development of the individual studio narrative leading to the creation of an aesthetic object. Many artists who work with diverse populations are self-taught to some degree. Working outside the academic and gallery culture, community artists pursue collaborative alternatives and create a wave of actions that has redefined art-making in the 21st century. Community artists tend to see art as an essentially democratic medium, available to everyone who is interested, instead of limited to traditional art audiences. These artists have discovered processes that allow and encourage impact and change in a society.

Over the past forty years, few colleges and universities offered social practice programs. Now, social practice art programs rooted in the efforts of these pioneering artists, are blossoming in colleges and universities across the country. Today's students are entering arts programs and universities with a heightened sense of societal responsibility and with an increased expectation of socially based experiences. These curricula and programs will be a major part of their education as they create a place for themselves in today's society and economy.

Many projects have underscored this fundamental shift in thinking. In 2011, a top New York gallery artist, Eric Fischl, became deeply involved in social artistic practice by creating *America: Now and Here*, a creative dialogue about America that mixed nationally known icons of contemporary art with the work of local artists. The concept focused on including non-arts audiences in the conversation by respecting their responses and providing them with collaborative creative voices. Cindy Sherman, Chuck Close, Jeff Koons and Tom Friedman are only a few from the long list of contributing artists.

Artworkers: Creativity and America

The Statue of Liberty in New York had a rough time in 2013. Hit by Superstorm Sandy, the monument re-opened July 4th, after millions of dollars were spent on repairing it. Originally a gift from the French, the figure referred to as Lady Liberty is actually named Liberty Enlightening the World. 2013 is the 127th anniversary of the statue.[2]

The idea of Liberty depicted as a woman, leading the populace on the path to expanded thinking, has been around for a while. One of the best historical examples is Eugene Delacroix's *Liberty Leading the People*, which was painted in 1830, in response to the French revolution. The heroine of Delacroix's piece leads a group of people through a shadowy frame toward enlightenment.[3]

Designed by Frederic Auguste Bartholdi, a French artist and sculptor, the Statue of Liberty was a collaborative effort between a man with an idea, an artist, two architects, three engineers, a publisher, many fundraisers, lawyers, and financial contributors from both France and the United States. One of the architects/engineers, Gustave Eieffel, was Bartholdi's teacher, as well as the designer of the Eiffel tower in Paris.[4] When funds for the statue ran out, publisher Joseph Pulitzer ran an appeal to raise money from the United States public, which was enthusiastically answered. In a powerful testimonial to the power of the people, sufficient funds were raised to continue the project through installation. In 1885, Pulitzer wrote this about the statue:

> *"… It is not a gift from the millionaires of France to the millionaires of America, but a gift of the whole people of France to the whole people of America."*[5]

Like many sections of the *ArtWorkers: Creativity and America* exhibition, the statue and the immense coordination required to secure its installation serve as a reminder of the importance of imparting knowledge. This exchange of learning

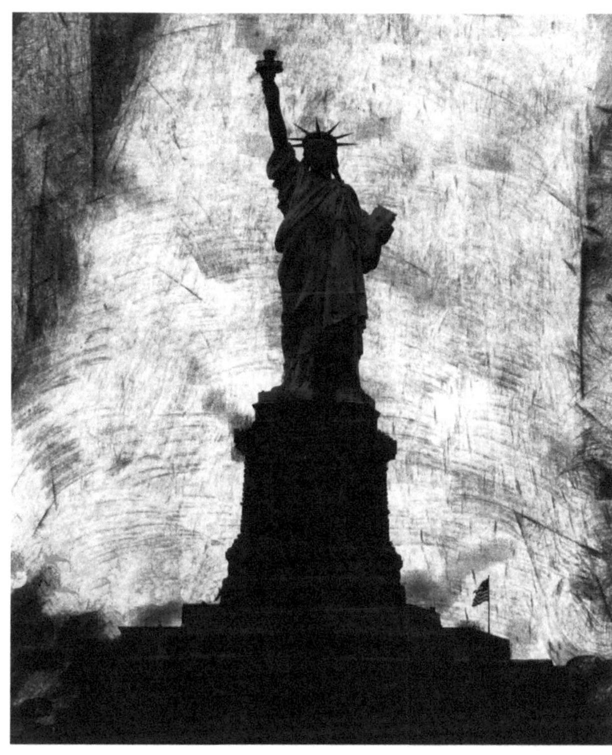

and making helps art move beyond traditional friends and supporters.

The exhibition, conceived by Hugh Merrill and presented at the George A. Spiva Center for the Arts in Joplin, Missouri, in the summer of 2013, posed questions reflecting on our country's past and present, while mirroring the mindset of a recovering Midwestern tornado town. An EF5 tornado hit Joplin in 2011, devastating the landscape and killing 161 people. Another tornado in Moore, OK resulted in far fewer deaths, even though the tornado itself was much larger.[6] Driving through certain parts of Joplin reveal a seemingly disproportionate number of brand-new brand-name stores and restaurants.

The tornado zone reflects an eerie nostalgia, reminiscent of the photography of Walker Evans or William Christenberry. Some of the half-remaining trees have objects trapped in broken branches that remain at the 2-year-anniversary of the event. A sober and reflective energy, the landscape asks "what if?" The trees suggest thoughts on the environment, where we are now, and the knowledge that situations that seem to be stable are instead, volatile.

Merrill has been interested in public participation since the 1980s, when he began promoting and exhibiting community-based work. Working with French conceptual artist Christian Boltanski in 1998, Merrill planned an exhibition at a restaurant in New York City, which later appeared at the Kemper Museum of Contemporary Art in Kansas City, MO. At the time, both artists were interested in different aspects of the general public. Boltanski was interested in people who had disappeared, and Merrill was investigating marginalized and displaced populations that were many times invisible to the rest of society. Through the *ArtWorkers* exhibition, Merrill's idea to give everyone in a region a voice has come full circle. One of the goals of the exhibition was to engage with a traditionally conservative community, encouraging a dialogue on the subject of America through prompts referencing icons and monuments.

Conceptually, the art produced by local artists and gallery attendees for the show ranged from one side to another: political and propaganda, history, nostalgia, environmental concerns, cross-dressing, human hybrids, youth and age, liberation, and re-purposed pianos represent a few of the elements involved. Events were well supported by dialogue through public events, workshops, musical performances and other activities.

The exhibition focused on portraits of many types. Everyone was welcome to have their photo taken in the *MIX UP: American Diversity* section of the exhibit. Prints of many faces were separated into three strips: eyes, nose and mouth. People held up these elements to their own faces and got an immediate makeover. All attendees were invited to have their picture taken with Merrill's vision of Lady Liberty, a large printed banner featuring the Statue of Liberty against an intense pink sky. Responses written on post-it

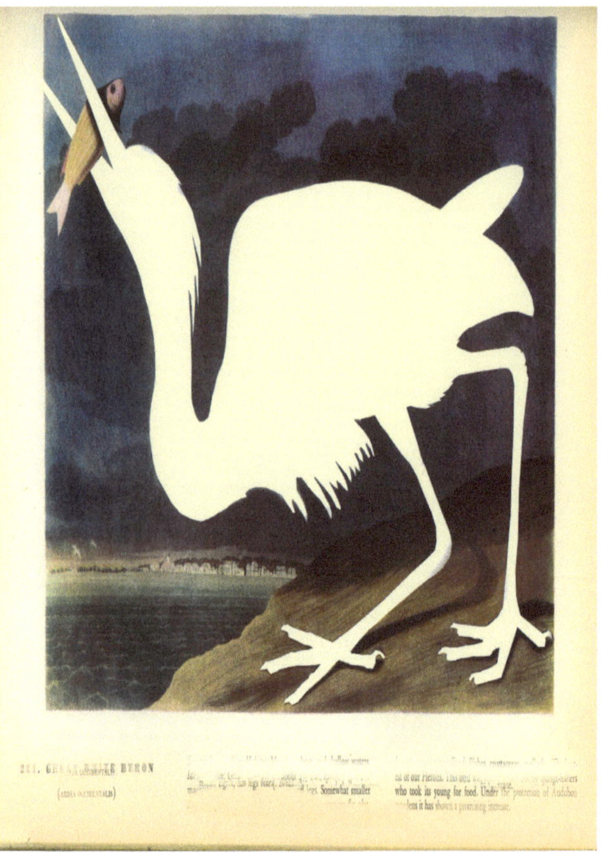

notes answer the question: "what do you want to be liberated from?" The answers varied:

- Religious or political references
- Everyday concerns
- Personal anxiety
- Perceived truths
- Global and environmental
- Family life
- Finances

Folks wanted liberation from: fracking, war, Obama, Obamacare, intolerancia, garbage, taxes, over-eating, fast food, Mizzou, time, idiots, gay bashing, pain of loss, sadness, inability to deal with anger and binge eating disorders. Others expressed the desire to be free of things such as depression, anxiety, the word "can't," debt, government, rain, the cops, guns, old age, school and school loans.

Historically, an interest in environmentalism began on an organized level in the early 1960s, but actually started thousands of years ago. As early as 6000 BCE deforestation resulted in the collapse of community in southern Israel.[7] In 1853, gold rush speculators downed a 300 foot tall, 1,244-year-old Sequoia tree in Calaveras County, California. When it was exhibited, a media and public outcry ensued. This was a watershed event that founded the conservation movement.[8]

Hugh Merrill has incorporated environmental concerns in his work from the time he was a student. Born in 1949, Merrill was thirteen when Rachel Carson released her book *Silent Spring* in 1962. An early reader of the work, he was interested in the ideas of damaged natural ecosystems and their effect on living birds, animals, and people. Merrill's Birds series, consisting of ten mixed media pieces, is an ongoing commentary utilizing images from John James Audubon's *Birds of America* series. Like Audubon, Merrill concentrates on meticulous studio practice, a mastery of media and materials, and a passionate belief in stewardship and observation.

Although environmentalism started with an emphasis on public health, it is now a much larger issue. Although we have clean air and water for our own personal use, we remain divorced from the majority of the pollution present outside of the spaces we live and work in. We now have to grapple with the task of the health of our earth, as well as our own. Merrill is concerned with environment as a spatial concept, as well as a physical and emotional plane.

Through an ongoing interest in current events, politics, and social justice, Merrill has been driven to seek conversation about the history of our country, as well as an open discussion of how other people feel about it.

At the opening reception, all age groups were represented. To the crowd's delight, Darth Vader and his storm troopers posed for photographs as they walked through the crowd. Thousands of people, artists and non-artists,

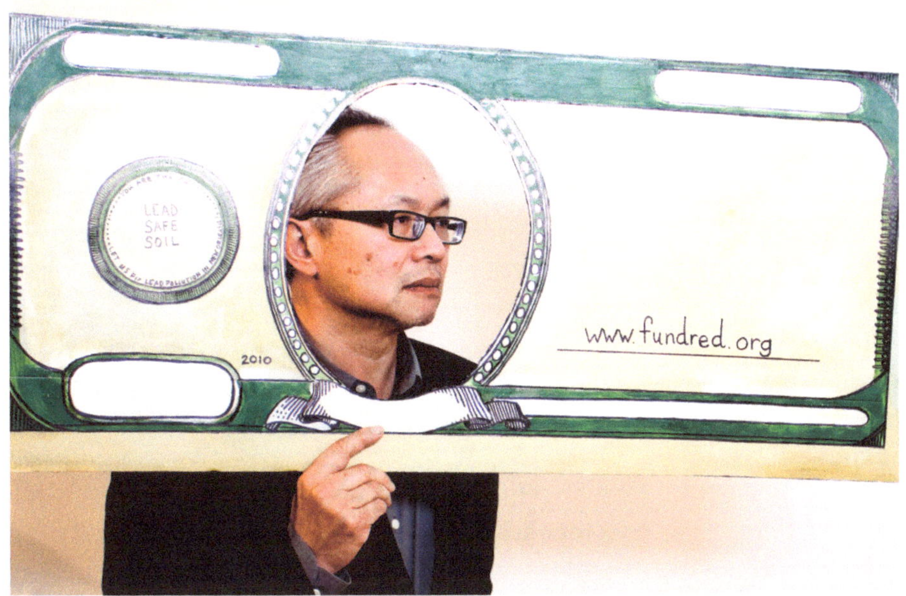

Mel Chin, *Fundred Dollar Bill Project*, 2010. Photo: Emmett Merrill.

combined to create a contemporary portrait of Joplin, two years after our nation's seventh deadliest tornado.[9] It is not surprising that the art speaks of darkness and anger as well as a quiet but determined optimism. More importantly, the viewpoints expressed are genuine, and not the visions of the artist or curator. Over the seven weeks that *ArtWorkers* continued, Merrill held workshops every Saturday, so the exhibition got larger as more people added their thoughts.

Engaging a rural, right-wing community in artistic expression and exhibition creates a number of challenges. Many people who live in the region are suspect of contemporary art in general, but others warmed quickly to the idea of a public voice.

The exhibition received a National Endowment for the Arts grant, as well as support from the Missouri Arts Council. Local businesses and individuals also contributed financially and through personal effort. The work is the largest event to date at the Spiva Center.

The Fundred Dollar Bill Project

Social practice projects can prove effective for engaging participants in social, political and economic themes. International artist Mel Chin's *Fundred Dollar Bill Project* works to make three-million Americans into artists by having them draw their own 100-dollar bills. These individually crafted pieces serve to raise creative capital for neighborhood cleanup in the city of New Orleans, Louisiana, a region infamous for high levels of pollution. Cleanup costs are estimated at about 300 million dollars.

Chin took his show on the road in 2010, stopping in art galleries and schools to recruit support for his project. Both his effervescent personality and his transportation, a bio-diesel powered armored car, drew lots of attention and fans along the journey. Upon the completion of 3 million works of art, Chin will present the pieces on the steps of the US Congress, in an attempt to convince them to exchange real money for the *Fundreds*.[10] Although the prospects for actually receiving cash are limited, *Fundreds* draws attention to the environment and the economy through the lens of creativity.

This project is in support of Chin's *Paydirt* event, which uses hyper-accumulating plants to pull pollutants out of soil. The project started with a small patch of land in Minnesota planted in conjunction with the Walker Art Center. Chin says the main impetus for the project is the children affected by the pollution "It's a visceral problem," he says. "It's in their bones, and in their brains."[11]

Both of these ambitious national projects follow the criterion for community-based art by placing the action and the outcome above aesthetic result. This criterion was developed by artists re-evaluating traditional studio practice and taking creativity and opinions out into the streets, beginning in the early 1980s. For these artists, art is not a search for absolute truth but is the ignition for community redefinition, protest, discussion, and the experience of creativity in everyday life through social practice.

First coined in 1996 by French art critic Nicolas Bourriaud, the term *relational aesthetics* stems from European creative practices related to the whole of human society immersed in social context.[12] The writings of American philosopher and educator John Dewey informed Bourriaud's work,[13] as Dewey also believed in experience-based learning and that learned experience provided empowerment, which allowed people to reach their societal potential.[14] Dewey was best known for his work to advance the fields of education and philosophy. Through his awareness of the differences in people, and how these differences change individual's ways of learning, Dewey came to believe in the prospect of personal growth through experience, education, and art.[15] Bourriaud expanded upon these ideas and brought them into a context relevant to contemporary art.

Bourriaud further discusses social interactions by referring to them as distraction: "Artistic activity is a game, whose forms, patterns, and functions develop and evolve according to periods of social contexts; it is not an immutable essence."[16]

Since the 1970s, art has been moving from the white walls of the museum to a place within the daily lives of diverse populations. Social practice grew out of the feminist art movement, social and conceptual sculpture, relational aesthetics, performance art happenings, Surrealism, Dada, project art and French post-modern philosophers Guattari and Deleuze.

What was once considered less than aesthetically pertinent has grown into a major consideration for artists, art schools, universities, and museum exhibitions. It has been a slow climb from "doing something good" to theoretical consideration leading to acceptance. The ascent toward relevancy was often hindered by narrow conceptions of what art is and who can be considered an artist. White males were disproportionately represented in both museums and galleries, while women, community members, minorities, LGBT and other artists began to write their own histories outside of the established art world.

In 1991, Mary Jane Jacob presented *Places with a Past: New Site-Specific Art* at the annual Spoleto Festival in Charleston, South Carolina. This world-class arts festival features contemporary fine art, music, theatre, and dance, as well as related performances and shows of various types. In the opening essay of the accompanying publication for the project, Jacob speaks of a new category of contemporary art called projects, which she sees as an effective move away from traditional gallery spaces.[17] Alternative settings add interest and character to the work. Site-specific sculptures were created by well-known artists at the time and produced with direct input from the community of in existing structures throughout the city.[18]

Each artist worked with a specific space to create a work impossible to re-create anywhere else. The works reflected both the vision of contemporary artists and the local flavor of the town. Directly related to relational aesthetics, this form of art addressed the rift between the artist and everyman and is a foundational source for social practice.

Chapter 3:
Criterion for Community Art: Underlying Construct

Nicolas Bourriaud has said:

"Art was invented to prepare and announce a future world; today, it is modeling possible universes . . . This 'chance' can be summed up in just a few words: learning to inhabit the world in a better way, instead of trying to construct it based on a pre-conceived idea of historical evolution."[1]

Social creative practice is concerned with experimental actions calling for interaction with viewers. The educational and studio activities are produced in collaboration with social, political and cultural discourse. These aspects are valued more than a purely aesthetic and visual experience. Relational arts actions are implicitly democratic structures, concentrating on participation and relevance to everyday life. Many times, the audiences for community works may not recognize themselves as artists, or the works themselves as art. Instead, they see the experiences as something else entirely, a coincidence or non-typical afternoon's activities.[2]

Artist Harrell Fletcher responds to the question "How did you perceive the 'normal course' while you were in school?" by saying:

"It's so concentrated in graduate school; you see all of these people going into their studios, spending hours and hours making objects or paintings. And it's supposed to be about isolating themselves. Maybe they have a wall of inspirational clippings from magazines, but that's the extent of their interaction with the world."[3]

Even art produced in an individual's studio, seemingly for the artist's self-expressive impulses, is ultimately a collective action. The art object is only completed when viewed by the eyes of the audience and validated as art by the art establishment and larger society. The actual meaning is forever derived from a bond to temporal perceptions and cultural influences. In this way, everything is new as viewed through the eyes, memory and values of each individual.

Artists in western society are expected to be insightful individuals with special abilities to help discover, challenge and expand our understanding of meaning, beauty and society. Social practice sidesteps this definition of an artist and shifts attention away from the individual to help us see potential creativity in others. Social artistic process places the artist in a new position, toggling between artistic vision, community organizing, public relations and anonymity. The artist goes beyond the architecture of the private studio space to form a shared creative space with available resources working toward a combined positive outcome.

The artist becomes something like a tribal shaman, speaking for and with the community as part of a ritual that helps to cement family, belief, faith and the other values. As pointed out in the mystical science of Kabbalah, all human acts, no matter how altruistic, are to a significant degree egotistical. Lucy Lippard says that "art as ritual reflects a nostalgia for times when art had significance in daily life."[4]

Historically, ritual has played an important role in religious and social interactions. Animal symbolism and self-identification is present in numerous civilizations, from pre-Columbian Mesoamerica to the plains tribes of North America, a belief in the energy and vitality of local animal personalities permeates art, history, and legend.

This could involve an individual dancer dressed in the mask of a deer, and embodying the spirit of the animal. The perceived self has the opportunity to disappear in the act of the ritual.

The artist in contemporary society has little chance to leave the self and ego behind, but they can come to balance the relationship between what is done for the self, and what is done for others. Giving one's time and effort to help other people provides more benefit for an individual on a spiritual and egotistical level than does receiving. Socially based art is not simplistic or egoless. The artist is giving to others using multiple levels of intellect, creative action, organizing and politics. While artists are providing knowledge and energy, they are also receiving in-kind knowledge and energy.

Artists Joseph Beuys, Amelia Mesa-Bains, Felix Gonzalez-Torres and David Hammons point out that pragmatism, materialism, superficiality and combativeness are all hallmarks of our dominant Anglo culture. These artists believe that art provides a revitalizing process for individuals and society. They reject the commercial, ego and celebrity-based aesthetics of mainstream art production and seek to reinvent art making based on like-minded values, actions and social justice.

Building on these perceptions, community work can be defined as a force that compels personal and social transformation through a combination of rituals and symbols that inspire emotional connections with shared experience. Art and artistic social practice are intertwined with ritual and audience engagement. Artists are social sculptors, using their expertise in theatrical and visual language to lead and facilitate expression, celebration and discourse. The results of many of these actions are not aesthetic in a traditional sense. Instead, they create a new method for people to see, experience and take action regarding their own culture that contrasts with mainstream definitions.

Suzanne Lacy, in her book *Mapping the Terrain: New Genre Public Art*, states:

"For the past three decades visual artists of varying backgrounds and perspectives have been working in a manner that resembles political and social activity but is distinguished by its aesthetic sensibility. Dealing with some of the most profound issues of our time -- toxic waste, race relations, homelessness, aging, gang warfare and cultural identity -- a group of visual artists has developed distinct models for an art whose public strategies of engagement are an important part of its aesthetic language. The source of these artworks' structure is not exclusively visual or political information, but rather an internal necessity perceived by the artist in collaboration with his or her audience."[5]

As arts programs in public schools are reduced or cut, the need for the arts does not diminish but increases. All children have the potential to benefit from arts processes that are proven to help them understand their lives and choices that they make by underscoring positive effects. Lacy frequently references violence or societal bloodletting to emphasize the healing effects of increasing one's self-awareness.[6]

In reflecting on the traditional art audience, David Hammons says:

"The art audience is the worst audience in the world. It's overly educated, it's conservative, it's out to criticize, not to understand, and it never has any fun. Why should I spend my time playing to that audience? The street audience is much more human, and their opinion is from the heart."[7]

Hammons' rise out of marginalized society to prominence in the mainstream art world is a testament to his commitment to social justice.

From politically incorrect to unpopular, his work runs the gamut of scathing criticisms of our hierarchical reality. Hammons' work is immersed with the ritualistic power of everyday objects such as gardening spades, bottles of cheap wine and other references to a capitalistic struggle for power over society through objectification.

Higher Goals (1986) was a statement about perception and ambition. In many low-income communities, sports are seen as a way to get out of a less-than-ideal life situation. By placing basketball goals on top of telephone poles, Hammons created a striking contrast of the perception of these objects. He wanted the audience to consider that goals are related to sports, but this is not their only function. Self-esteem, self-awareness and the ability to move forward in one's own life are also directly related to setting personal goals.[8]

German conceptual artist Joseph Beuys came of age in WWII Germany. He fought in the war and afterward directly benefited from the healing qualities of art. Beuys believed everyone was an artist, and he was an influential member of the Fluxus group, which was formed in opposition to Abstract Expressionism. Beuys and his fellow artists successfully re-invented the avant-garde after the war was over. Beuys specifically was intensely focused on everyday items, and the non-traditional symbolic and metaphorical use of materials, including animals.[9]

He once said: "Only art is capable of dismantling the repressive effects of a senile social system that continues to totter along the death line." He felt that art represents a heightening of humanitarian culture, which he saw as directly linked to social commentary and political activism. Beuys was a founding member of Germany's Green Party.[10]

Felix Gonzales-Torres was a Cuban born artist whose work parallels Bourriaud and Rirkrit Tiravanija, an artist also known for his efforts in the field of relational aesthetics. Torres was more interested in the abstraction of space and the application of everyday life to exhibitions. Torres passed away in 1996, but his work continues to be exhibited all over the world. His connection with relational aesthetics and the ability to slice and dice forms as well as see their parallel relationships underscores the importance of his work.

The work of Dr. Eric Avery is an example of the results Gonzales-Torres and Beuys demand. Avery is an interesting character, as he is both a medical doctor and a visual artist, frequently using the medium of printmaking. In 1995, Avery silk-screened wallpaper with images from condom packages to demonstrate how to put a condom on a penis.[11]

The project was produced in conjunction with Houston's Contemporary Art Museum's *Wallpaper Works*. Museum staff installed the wallpaper in coffee shops and nightclub bathrooms frequented by the local LGBT community. The artwork was meant to both remind and inform people about AIDS. The goal of the work was to encourage changing established bad habits that would lead to contagion and death. In February 1996 at Brasil, one of the installation sites, a mother and her 10-year-old daughter were using the bathroom. The mother was shocked to see the directions, displayed with images of a condom and an erect penis. She made a complaint to the authorities, and the project made the regional news. When asked about the project, Avery stated he did not mean for the project to offend anyone, and he felt it was important to educate people about how both male and female condoms can be used to stop the spread of disease.[12]

Rick Lowe is the founder of Project Row Houses, a non-profit arts and cultural organization that works to help people foster creativity within their own spaces in Houston, Texas. Lowe has helped these neighborhoods go from dangerous and filled with crime and drugs, to beautiful places that support self-esteem and economic stability.[13]

Like many artists, Lowe was originally inspired by local children from the neighborhood who expressed an interest in a related but different project, inspiring him to move outside his comfort zone in the studio and into the area that would become Project Row Houses. He is interested in both the people as well as the history of the area. By making a commitment to a specific space, he is able to create meaningful, life-changing work outside the established art hierarchical system.[14]

Like Mary Jane Jacobs, Lowe is interested in both preserving properties and giving a nod to regional history by thinking about place in a manner that recalls and celebrates the inhabitants of the space. PRH is not about the houses, but it focuses on teaching people to live in a positive manner.

Augusto Boal's *Theatre of the Oppressed* has reached tens of thousands of people around the world and provided them a method to change their relationships to their oppressors through theatre performance. By expressing themselves through performance and dance, participants are able to explore their feelings and to work to channel negatives into positives within their lives. Boal sees the language of theatre as a universal language with which anyone can join in conversation.[15]

All of the artists mentioned above have a belief in the intuitive creative potential of what Hammons refers to as "Everyday people and the ability of art to fundamentally change the way these individuals perceive and act in their communities." The artists engaging as social critics and activists believe that art is simultaneously a spiritual and a political action meant to create a possibility for change.

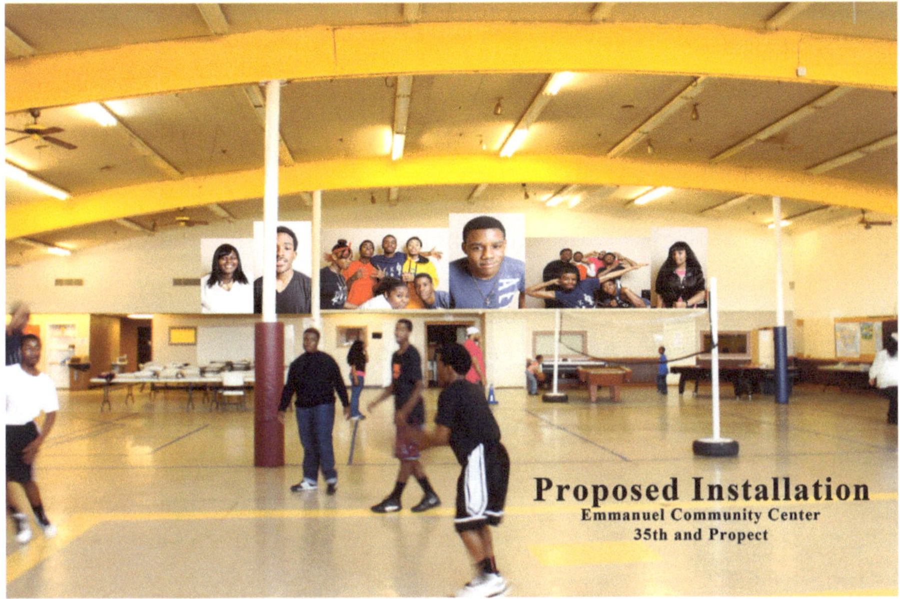

Proposal for interior of old grocery/ Emmanuel Community's Center, Kansas City Missouri, 2013.

Chapter 4:
What Do We Mean By a Criterion for Community Art?

Disciplinary art forms such as printmaking, sculpture and photography have identified a theoretical framework unique to their practice based on function, process and materials. In printmaking, artist and writer Ruth Weisberg defines the criterion for print as ink, pressure and paper.[1] This criterion provides a guide for evaluating, defining and classifying art activities. The terms defining community art and social practice are at best vague, and they overlap concurrent ideas about public art, percent-for-art projects, art in situ and guerrilla art actions. They also overlap and have the potential to redirect the function and value of traditional creative and artistic practices into new publicly accessible forms.

In the mid 1990s, writer, curator and activist Lucy Lippard pointed to an art that went beyond the stereotypical "art for the people," taking the universal language of abstraction to a more modest position in which art strives for local context and cultural authenticity, effectively becoming part of the fabric of the collective and asking artists to expedite, listen and work effectively with others. This type of art is inside the participants, as it is no longer limited to outside influences.[2]

The involvement of a trained professional artist who has special knowledge of visual and theatrical language legitimizes the relationship between art-making and social activism. The participation of a socially validated artist in the role of acknowledged expert contributes to the activity becoming art and not a protest, festival or other type of celebration.

Professors Beth Krensky and Seana Lowe Steffen, in their book, *Engaging Classrooms and Communities Through Art: A Guide to Designing and Implementing Community-Based Art Education,* describe the need for professional artists:

> *"From a sociological perspective, an artist working in the social realm represents the institutions of the art world, legitimized by society to define the norms of creative interaction and the standards of artistic expression. Applied to the construct of art as ritual with the power to invoke and demarcate change, an artist can be thought of as having the authority role, comparable to that of a ritual elder or specialist facilitating ritual."*[3]

A criterion based on the thoughts, ideas and concerns above creates a useful framework to understand and classify socially relevant art in relationship to more traditional modes of artistic production. The items that form this criterion are not carved in stone -- they are not laws or rules. The ideas function as a guidepost to allow individuals and organizations to distinguish and recognize the territory. This approach helps them to understand the context and goals of creative activity:

- Socially based art is functional; is it not purely aesthetic.
- Artistic ideas are not imposed on the participants, but are derived from direct interaction between artists and others.
- The artworks are created from time and experience in the field.
- Social practice is the beginning of a transformation from a fractured society into a communal society.
- Actions are rooted in accuracy and advocacy, with an outcome that arouses the public to bring about social change.
- Creativity and imagination are the first steps for envisioning and moving toward a better future by breaking hegemonic thinking and challenging barriers of the status quo.
- Art is validated by local cultural and social context.
- Projects allow people to engage in public spaces as well as engaging with each other.
- Art actions may lead to political action.
- Art nurtures a lost intuitive process.
- These methods dictate healing and provide new grounding for ethical, social and spiritual insight.
- Community practice is a process that fosters awareness and is a celebration of others' aliveness, which functions to move human potential from a static nature to a dynamic force for change.
- Arts projects create ripple effects that continue over time.

For the artist, teacher, social worker or anyone creating and facilitating arts actions, the criterion is open to change and evolution, and can even be tossed out. Creativity can never be defined and held within set boundaries. There are innumerable interdisciplinary bridges and hidden pathways that go beyond the above criterion for community art. It is valuable to learn, forget, and relearn.

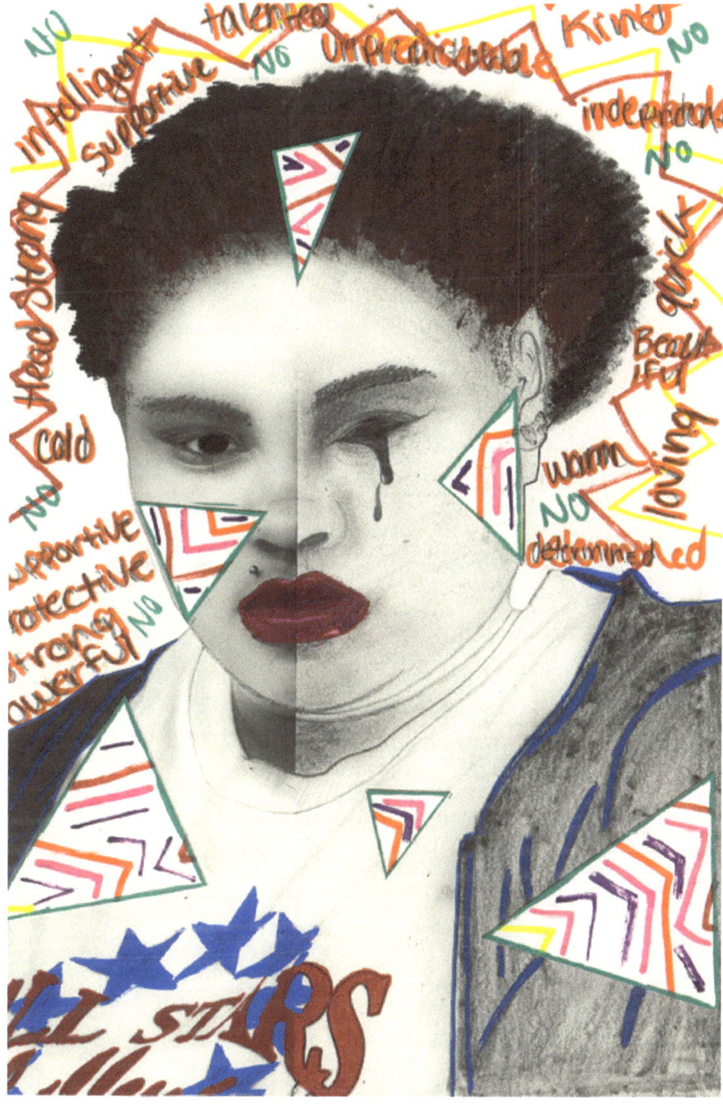

Haley Hatch and Chameleon Arts, *Ghost Drawing*, Emmanuel's Community Center, Kansas City, Missouri, 2013.

Chapter 5:
Teaching Fundamentals of Social Arts Practice

"The only thing we have to do to be sure we will leave a ruined world for our children and grandchildren is to do exactly what we are doing now."

-- James Gustave Speth, Dean of Forestry and Environmental Studies at Yale University[1]

Paper or Plastic?

The decision-making process that will determine not only our individual futures, but the futures of most all plants, animals and sentient beings on earth, has become impossible to ignore. It is not possible for anyone to remain uninvolved. We have entered a new age where our decisions and actions as individuals and a society will determine our very existence.

In the arts, teaching students to create their own private visual language at the expense of participation in the broader social realm is foolish and short-sighted. Teaching the values of social practice is relevant to all creative disciplines and is not a secondary concern. There is a fundamental need to engage and influence students to participate in life beyond their own memories, experiences and short-term aspirations. We have moved beyond the world of me to the world of us.

This reality is not the end of personal poetry or the studio narrative. The change is where they are placed in relation to the problems and concerns of the outside world. In the past paradigm, artists often excluded themselves from society, moving away form politics, science, social movements, religion and other currents that shaped society. Historically the studio functioned as architectural separation from the everyday world. By protecting the artist from the mundane, he or she would be able to discover deeper human meaning and reality. Where the problems of the world were tangential to the work of Jackson Pollock, they were central to Jose Gonzales-Torres. In a world where our individual actions combine to determine our collective ability to reach a green and sustainable collective, the artist is no longer peripheral to environmental and political concerns. The border of the self is no longer closed, it is open to and intermeshed with the society we live in.

There are fundamentals to teaching socially engaged art, and like most basic principles, they are different from the process of being an artist. Playing the horn as deftly as Chet Baker or Louie Armstrong is different from learning to play the trumpet. In the traditional arts college or university program, the student is given an assignment. The assignment can as open-ended as "Go make a drawing," or as narrow as "Make a logo for a new soft drink." In either case, the art student goes inside themselves, contacting their imagination to come up with the solution, works individually and is responsible for the final outcome of their piece. We call this the studio narrative, and it is a highly valued and important creative journey between the artist and their materials, ideas and processes. The studio narrative is a dialogue in which the maker responds to the forms being made.

Many times artists are only partially in control of their work, both in terms of understanding and creating. The creative process is a dialogue. Many non-artists are surprised to find that the artist has little specific knowledge of what the final outcome of their work will be. They assume that the artist sees the final image in their imagination and then proceeds to make it. There is an underlying assumption that art-making is divided into two parts: a vision, and a separate step to actually make the vision into a work of art.

The non-artist evaluates the work from their personal observation of the exhibited piece, so they are often unaware of the hidden journey that lies below the final layer of imagery they view in the gallery. They see the final image, but the studio narrative that took place to make the work is not on their radar.

The audience views the object through the habit of trying to comprehend, to decipher meaning, and attempting to understand the picture or form they are viewing using logic and language. They seldom get to enter into the vague, right-brained, intuitive creative process that ultimately enabled the artist to make the work.

Making and observing are fundamental to artistic and creative intelligence. Historically, society prizes the unique artistic vision and creative genius of the individual. In the late 1940s and into the 1950s, New York art critic Clement Greenberg championed Abstract Expressionism, a testosterone-fueled celebration of paint dipped in machismo. Jackson Pollock, Willem DeKooning and others formed this first significant American art movement.[2] Greenberg believed that great art was produced by individual genius, and it was this theory that put him on the map, even though it was considered controversial from the beginning. Fairfield Porter once said that his commitment to figurative painting was made to spite Greenberg.[3]

Interestingly, Pollock's wife, Lee Krasner, was also a pioneer in the flat, patterned imagery that became so valuable to the Abstract Expressionists. Her fundamental contribution to the world of art was recognized decades after her ideas influenced an entire generation of iconic male artists. Hans Hoffman, Willem De Kooning and Mark Rothko became some of the most influential Abstract Expressionists of the time period. Many artists in the feminist art movement made contributions as important as Krasner's, and were also recognized much later. The work of many of the abstract expressionists reflects the continuation of an interest in automatism, started by the Dadaists and continued by the Surrealists.[4]

Even though Greenberg's theories were largely put aside shortly after they were expressed, they have a proven staying power when applied to education. Artists, like everyone else, exist within a larger society that soaks them with influence on a daily basis. The involvement of all artists within a larger cultural framework proves to disrupt Greenberg's ideas, so the field of social practice can be viewed as the opposite pole to the Greenbergian studio narrative.

Feminist writer Linda Nochlin held a different perspective, when she said:

> *"The problem lies not so much with some feminists' concept of what feminist art is– but rather, with their misconceptions– shared with the public at large–of what art is: with the naïve idea that art is the direct, personal, expression of individual emotional experience, a translation of life into visual terms. Art is almost never that, great art never is."*[5]

Nochlin also believed that an established patriarchal art world hierarchy prevented women artists from succeeding. She saw it as a problem embedded in institutions. "Disadvantage may be an excuse," she said. "It is not, however, an intellectual position."[6] Nochlin and her contemporaries established an alternative to the established art historical canon. By chronicling the work of the West Coast feminist movement in the 1970s and 1980s they created a place where the hierarchical art world had lost much of it's relevance.

Prioritizing Greenberg's method of creative investigation, art schools direct students to develop a vision based on a private narrative. Eventually, the artwork is brought to the audience through exhibition -- either in a gallery, or another venue. In art school, this process takes place when the student brings their creation to class for critique by their peers and faculty. From this critical input, the artist/student goes back into the solitary studio and individually re-thinks, re-creates and varies their work. The work is subsequently brought back for another critique and further development. This system of creation supports personal poetry and the individual genius of the maker. Authorship, ownership, and copyright all belong to the individual artist.

In community art, the studio narrative is turned on its head, so personal poetry is placed at the end of the process or may not even exist as a viable outcome. Artists must go outside themselves prior to working and must facilitate rather than express. They must engage others and help them to establish their voice, rather than articulating their own individualism. The process of social practice is collaborative and non-hierarchical. Quick judgment of the aesthetic value of the work is not relevant, as the work articulates the authenticity of multiple voices. Where studio art can sometimes be critiqued as contrived or forced, socially based art has an undeniable authenticity that creates cultural value.

To work effectively with others, artists must first immerse themselves within a community, learning to understand their lives, perceptions, and viewpoints. The process of getting to know and experiencing people can be the source of the art itself.

An example of an immersion project is Hugh Merrill's percent-for-art work at the Sanford-Kimpton Health Center in Columbia, Missouri, which stared in 2002 and was completed in 2004. He collected people's personal stories, photographs, and other personal memorabilia from the center's staff and other local folks using the clinic. From this mass of personal information, Merrill created large-scale graphic collages that were digitally printed and installed throughout the various departments in the building. The images acted as art to the broader public that visited the facility, but for the staff the art works represented their cherished family photographs and memories.

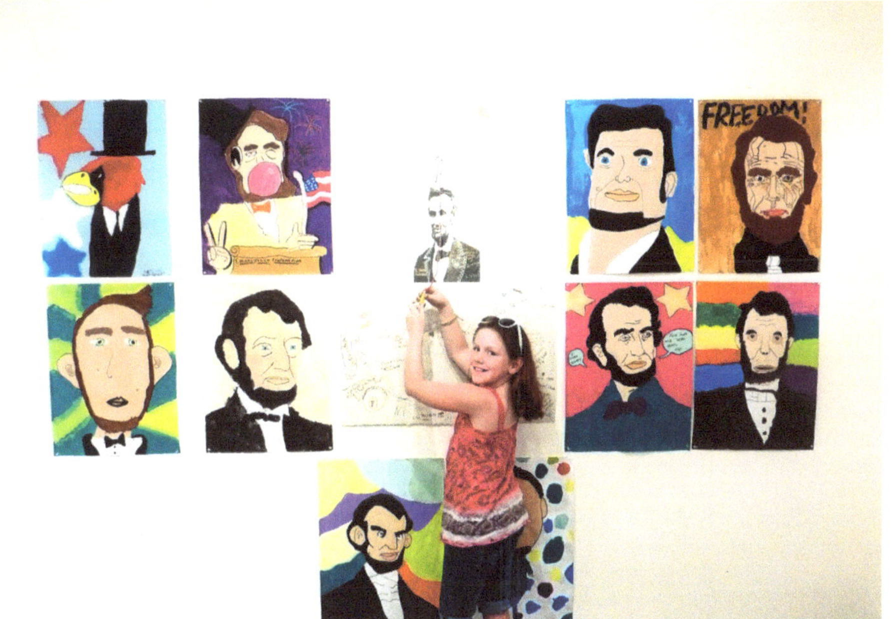

Finding Lincoln at *Artworkers: Creativity and America*, at the George A. Spiva Art Center, Joplin, Missouri, 2013

Chapter 6:
Roles of the Artist and Community

The role of a community artist is clear in traditional studio practice; they are all responsible for the creation of a unique artwork. The role of an artist is fundamentally that of a collaborator. The lines between artist and subject are blurred, and authorship of the work is plural, rather than individual. There are many ways to work together and many levels of interaction that guide the artist in the creation of a public artwork or project. In this section, the roles of the artist are presented as a series of possibilities. The roles move from hands-off to hands-on. There are innumerable shades of participation an artist or arts group can take in creating and facilitating social projects. There is no hierarchy in the way they are listed, one approach is not better than the other. Each is a valid position from which to facilitate and participate in a project.

Artist, Catalyst, Guide.

These are three terms that describe how an artist or group might provide creative, technical, and management support for a project. They provide a concept and structure but do not intervene to alter the expressive voice of the artist or student.

Since the 1970s, photographer Wendy Ewald has collaborated with children, families, women and teachers in countries across the globe, including Saudi Arabia, India and Mexico. Ewald's projects use photography to probe questions of identity and cultural differences, exploring a theme that will be the topic of the photographs.[1]

The participants then create the artwork without intervention. Ewald helps the children or adults with any technicalities or media questions they have. The art-making itself is in the hands of the natural creative ability of the children. In Mexico, some of the kids photographed their dream world, and in North Carolina they explored neighborhoods and the concept of being the "other." When the photos were returned to the classroom, the works were discussed and poetry or ideas were recorded about them. Ewald's role changes significantly after the pieces are finished. She quickly becomes a curator as opposed to a teacher.[2]

Beyond her artistic and curatorial roles, Ewald has had to take on administrative activities that call for non-artistic skills. Working with local schools, city managers, churches, embassies and other social institutions, she interfaces with the people involved to give the work a life outside the classroom, many times in the form of a formal exhibition. Prior to visiting with the children, she has had to raise funds, write grants and make contact with a variety of cultural and educational institutions to support the project. After that, there is the packaging and dissemination of the artwork to a broad international audience.

Ewald often makes her own photographs while working with various communities. She will invite the children to draw and write on her negatives, creating works of dual authorship. This collaborative process disrupts the traditional hierarchy of artist to subject, twisting the two strands into a single thread. It also demonstrates the use of multiple approaches to the arts action, as she takes on the roles of both facilitator and participating artist.

In the early 1980s, Tim Rollins received a small National Endowment for the Arts grant to produce a program for kids in the New York Public School system. It was set up as an after-school program for children who had been determined to be at-risk. Many had been essentially written off by the system due to anti-social behavior, learning disabilities or other circumstances. This original group soon dubbed themselves "Kids of Survival," and working directly with Rollins, they now have work in the permanent collections of most major museums in the United States.[3]

Rollins and KOS worked frequently with literary themes. Melville's *Moby Dick* and Kafka's *Amerika* are two of their best-known works. It has been said about Rollins: "He was always a teacher, it was part of his personality."[4] Over 30 years later, Rollins continues his work with KOS. He is a great example of someone whose commitment to collaboration has made a significant difference in the lives of the participants and an immense contribution to the history of art in general.

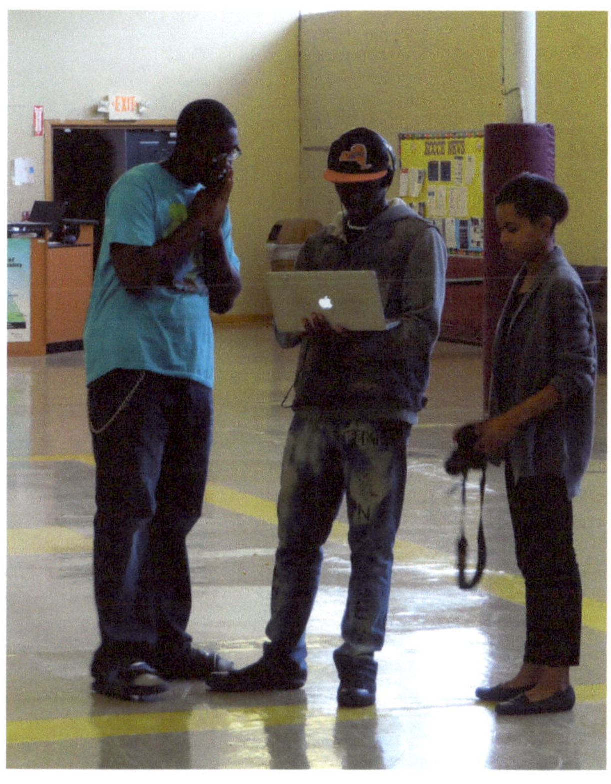

Left: *Insights*, facilitated by Lauren McGill at Emmanuel's Community Center, Kansas City, Missouri, 2014.

Below: Collaborative portraits at Emmanuel's Community Center, Kansas City, Missouri, 2013.

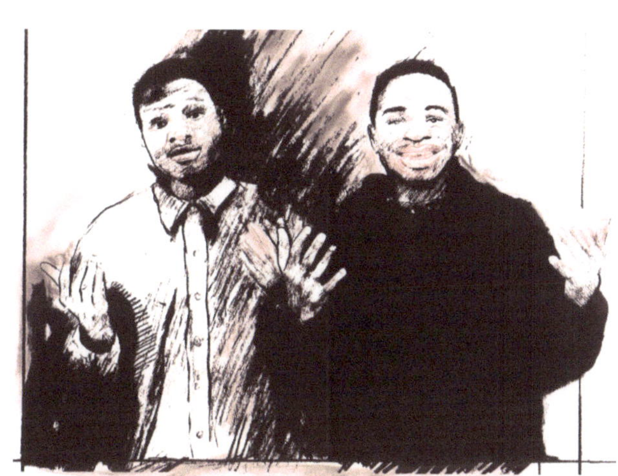

Artist Collaborator

The artist collaborator goes beyond setting the conceptual tone for a project. They not only facilitate the project, but actually take part in the creation of the work. This is a hands-on approach to creating the final work. Although the artist is involved as a participant, collaboration is the lifeblood of the process and final project. The artist has the participants produce the resources that will become the content and visual material from which the final work will be made, using their expertise and knowledge to translate the communities input into a coherent work of art.

So Yeon Park, an associate professor at the University of Kansas in Lawrence, Kansas, produced *Storytelling and Listening* in partnership with Chameleon Arts and Youth Development. The Office of Homeless Liaison from the Kansas City, Kansas, Public School District also participated in the project.

From 2003-2005, CAYD worked with a group of homeless middle and high school students to assist in the development of basic academic skills. In 2005, Park designed the *Storytelling and Listening* curriculum. Each Saturday for 12 weeks, she met with a group of 30 homeless children and asked them to create drawings that documented their daily lives, dreams, hopes and fears. The original drawings were done on letter-sized sheets of paper with black Sharpie markers. Park collected the drawings and scanned them into the computer in her studio. She then printed the drawings as quilt squares and created a 12-foot wide circular white quilt with black line drawings utilizing the square design. When the quilt was completed, she set up an installation and performance with the children in a black box theatre at the local YWCA.

The children pulled the quilt over their legs and sat in a circle. Park set up a video camera to both record the activity and project it onto a large screen. The children passed around a microphone, giggled, laughed and told stories about the drawings and how they related to their everyday lives. The

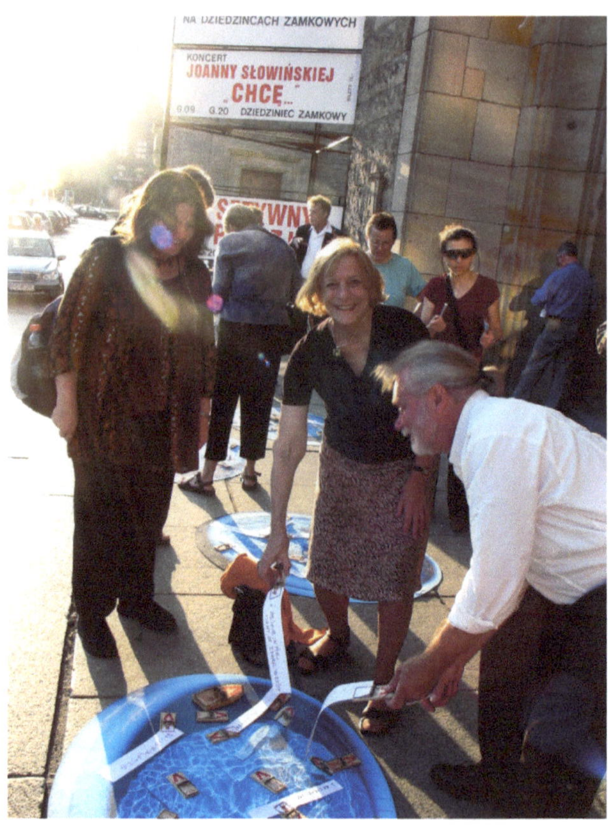

Hugh Merrill, *Pools of Belief*, public art installation in Posnan, Poland, 2005.

quilt and the video were exhibited at the Museum of Contemporary Art in Seoul, Korea.

There is a wonderful balance between the collaborative action and the artistic production of the quilt and video in *Storytelling and Listening*. The children shared their stories with candid enthusiasm and became excited when they learned the piece would be exhibited in a country on the other side of the world. Park's collaboration validated the complex lives of these homeless children. The very act of an outsider becoming invested in their experiences was highly meaningful to the kids.

Often the process of making art, writing, drawing, photographing or singing breaks through the child's boundary of fear and negative participation. Homeless, at-risk, and adjudicated youth populations are often wounded and highly self-destructive. Many simply do not believe in their own value, so it is difficult for them to overcome the gravity of their own life.

The artist can help to break this cycle of self-destruction by producing work that increases personal value and honors their experiences. The homeless children So Yeon Park worked with were all living on the edge of gang violence, drugs and self-destructive choices about school and life. The CAYD arts program in general, and *Storytelling and Listening* specifically, helped these kids to overcome the fires they faced in moving forward with their lives. One of the children is now a graduate of Drake University; others have attended local community colleges and started families. Without the artist interventions, their path would have been even more dangerous and difficult.

Artist in Public

The word artist comes before the word public because work is produced by an individual working directly with local folks. The artist may be a member of the group they work with, so they are connected in a common culture. The experience shared between the artist and the participants helps to determine the scope, content, and direction of the project.

The final work represents, speaks to, informs, confronts and celebrates the people who came together and made the work possible. The final product is marked by the artist's individual insight and vision. In many cases, the first audience is the group participating, and the secondary audience is the art gallery patrons, and the broader art world. In 2011, a group of students in the community art and service learning class at the Kansas City Art Institute designed *Random Acts of Kindness*, a project to enliven the routines of people catching the bus at the corner of 31st St. and Troost Avenue in Kansas City, Missouri. Troost is the historical dividing line between the African-American and white working-class neighborhoods in Kansas City. The folks riding the bus were served coffee on cold winter mornings and given apples for snacks. Some of the students set up a book exchange, while others collected stories of the riders and photographically documented the project. Some of the photographs were blown up into large digital posters celebrating the folks at the bus stop. The posters were installed in windows of nearby abandoned storefronts where the riders could see their images.

Prayer is an activity that can take place in private, or in public. Kansas City artist Dylan Mortimer makes it easier for people to choose the public option. Since 2003, Mortimer has exhibited his Prayer Booths across the country. Designed to mimic actual phone booths in appearance, the cubicles feature graphics in the form of classically styled praying hands inspired by German master Albrecht Dürer. They are phone-booth light-blue in color, which makes them easily recognizable to people who appreciate or once used public phones.

Historically, art and religion have been intimately intertwined. Religious art was many times didactic and specific, making tactical points on belief and establishing an institutional reference for the faithful. Mortimer understands the relationship between religion and society. He creates a parallel space where even people who don't usually think about religion can see an interesting change in the energy surrounding a sacred place unique to their existence. Part of the mystic appeal is the reference to the once-popular phone booths, but this is clearly something else. This work functions as an acknowledgment or statement of suggestion.

When asked about the public's reaction to the pieces, Mortimer says:

> *"The public's reaction has been all over --love, hate, people use them sincerely, jokingly, some are mad because they thought they were real phone booths. There has been vandalism--Lawrence was the worst... [In] many cities there have been groups or organizations that have tried to have them removed. In NYC I received physical threats and death threats...."*

Mortimer's collaboration with religion serves as a catalyst, bringing his work into public focus very quickly. The audience's interaction immediately becomes part of the ongoing narrative of the piece. It functions autonomously, without a specific church, or a preacher. Direct public feedback isn't always evident in socially relevant work, and many times its effect is obscured. The use of cultural references in these pieces illustrates how the audience can be unwittingly involved in a cultural statement.[5]

Collaborative Political Art Intervention

It has been said the American mainstream can be marked by apathy and denial. This should not surprise us. Although 9/11, wars in Iraq and Afghanistan, followed by the great recession should have woken up the country, we continue to follow and support policies that sustain the status quo.

Even more distressing are proposed policies that would take us back in time, challenging progress in civil rights, women's rights, gay rights and environmental protection. Artists groups have a history of consistently and successfully challenging the power structures that destroy democracy, worker rights, and control the economy for the benefit of the one percent. The military industrial complex and war for profit are also frequently referenced. A massive influx of corporate spending in local and national elections has the potential to change the dynamic by which our democracy functions. Employers now take the right to tell their employees how to vote.

Historically, arts groups have come together to force change in society. Artists Meeting for Cultural Change, Artists and Writers Protest Against the War in Vietnam, Art Workers Coalition, Group Material and the Guerrilla Girls are all examples. Not only have they used art to protest, they have established a process of validation for collaborative creative arts practice. The doors to a new paradigm have been opened. Art can focus on issues and local solutions for families.

There is a price for free speech and artistic activism. Individual artists and arts groups have often been targeted by police, federal, and security agencies for their work, even though the investigations rarely lead to any findings of actual crime. The story of the Critical Arts Ensemble and Steven Kurtz shows the myopic vision and fear that led to the passage and enforcement of the Patriot Act.

Artist Steven Kurtz, who founded the critically acclaimed Critical Art Ensemble was working on a project in conjunction with the Massachusetts Museum of Contemporary Art, when his wife passed away from heart failure in 2004.[6]

Preparation for the exhibit involved themes of modified biology, and the Kurtz apartment contained a lab set-up to be used at the museum that raised the suspicion of local police. Suspected of biological terrorism by the FBI, Kurtz was detained while federal agents raided his apartment and confiscated his property.

After a full day in detention, it was determined by the New York State Commissioner of health that nothing in the home posed a threat of any kind. The reality that Hope Kurtz had passed away from natural causes was also accepted.[7]

Kurtz was not exonerated, as he was indicted on charges of mail and wire fraud later that year. Dr. Robert Farrell, a genetics professor at the University of Pittsburgh, was also charged. The charges concerned the mailing and purchase of harmless bacteria, and the relationship between the two men accused. Many of Kurtz's installation pieces included these bacteria.[8]

A series of stressors, including lymphoma, led to Ferrell's pleading guilty to misdemeanor charges in 2007, which his family opposed. He suffered a series of strokes after his indictment, and he was later sentenced to a year of unsupervised release and fined $500.00.

In April of 2008, Kurtz was finally vindicated when a judge determined that no crime had been committed, and the charges against him were dropped.[9]

When people say that art has little or no effectiveness in changing real world issues, they underestimate its importance and function. Art is deeply involved, on multiple levels, in the production of information, images, messages, and their dissemination into culture. The arts provide a grass roots, individual network for people to speak out on and pressure society to change.

Image-making is now possible for everyone with a cell phone, as witnessed by the Arab Spring and other social media based movements. Advancing technologies allow us to follow arts actions and persecutions in real time. The Gao Brothers and Ai Weiwei, all of whom are persecuted by the Chinese government, are excellent examples.[10] Chinese artists frequently use social media to invite guests to openings and events, helping them to exhibit under the radar and away from the authorities.

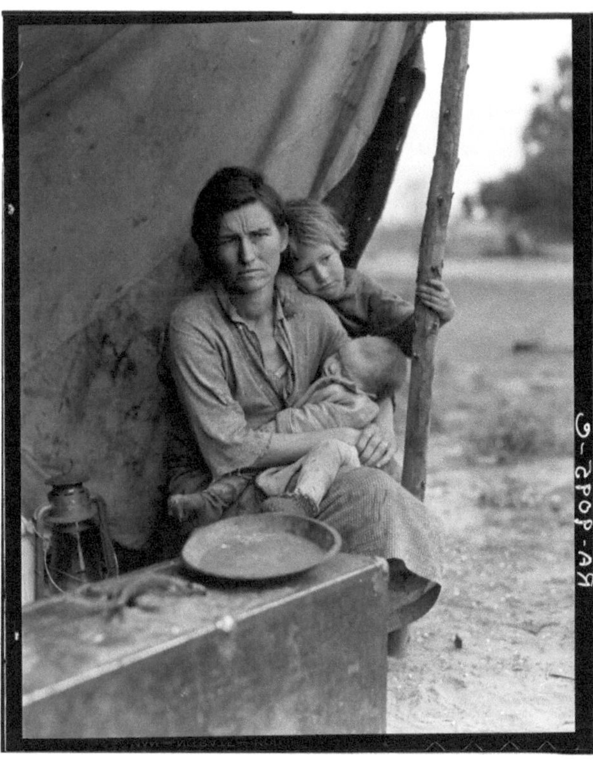

Dorothea Lange, *Migrant agricultural worker's family. Seven hungry children. Mother aged thirty-two. Father is native Californian. Nipomo, California*, 1936.

Documentary Artist

Documentary artistic practice is deeply rooted in photography, which represents a major stream of creativity in contemporary history and theoretical development. Dating back to the 1930s Works Project Administration, photographers established the core criterion for documentary consideration.[11]

Walker Evans, Dorothea Lange, Russell Lee, Marion Post Wolcott and others photographed Americans in their homes and local environments during the great depression. The images have become iconic symbols of the effects of poverty. Dorothea Lange's *Migrant Mother*, is a photograph of a woman who is 32 years old. She looks to be nearly 50. This example of a random American family serves to illustrate the desperation and heartbreak when a capitalistic system fails and then resets.

Carrie Mae Weems uses both actual historical photographs as well as staged scenes that have the same feel, as in her *Kitchen Table Series* (1990). Weems is interested in how African-Americans are viewed and how their historical roles are established. She is interested in what is behind a documentary photograph and how it becomes a final exhibition piece.[12] Weems frequently adds text to her photographs and installations, adding opinions that reject convention in favor of provocation. The work explores stereotypes and draws attention to social injustice. Her use of self-portraiture is a reminder that we cannot completely leave our own circumstances and our idiosyncratic opinions and reflections. What we can do is carefully consider our perceptions and contemplation of others, so we can begin to appreciate the intricacies of their views.

Historically, documentary photography has drawn attention to the circumstances of others, by illustration and reflection. Many important social movements have started with an image of injustice.

Street Artists

Graffiti artists and buskers (street performers) represent art forms that take place in public spaces, often without permission, and are created in a clandestine manner. These forms of street art are considered to be criminal acts in most communities, and it has been said that they contribute to the decline of communities, loss of businesses, and the destruction of neighborhoods.

Simultaneously, graffiti based art was valued quite highly by contemporary art galleries and museums. The exhibition Art from the Streets, put on by the Museum of Contemporary Art in Los Angeles, CA, in the fall of 2011, was the largest museum showing of graffiti art to date. It celebrated Cholo Tagging, the work of Swoon, Shepard Fairey, Banksy, Scribe and others. Writer Robert Atkins aptly defines graffiti art and its history in an article in *Artspeak: A Guide to Contemporary Ideas, Movements and Buzzwords*. *Graffito* means "scratch" in Italian, and graffiti (the plural form) are drawings or images scratched into the surfaces of walls.

Graffiti became an artistic consideration after World War II. Artists such as Cy Twombly and Jackson Pollock were interested in the line quality and general look of the work, while French artist Jean Dubuffet saw graffitists as outsiders, which he found intriguing.[13] The words and "tags" (graffiti writers' names) were soon coupled with elaborate images inspired by media and entertainment. Most graffitists were neither professional artists nor art students.[14]

Predictably, they were adventurous teenagers from the Bronx and Brooklyn. New York tagger Samo was also known as Jean-Michel Basquiat, who had the benefit of a middle class upbringing in Brooklyn. The Samo project was a collaboration with a high school friend, and when it was finished, they posted a piece announcing "Samo is dead." In the early 1980s, Basquiat soared to international success as a Neo-Expressionist and primitivist painter. Despite the carefully cultivated mirage of simplicity, Basquiat knew and enjoyed the company of many highly revered artists including Andy Warhol, with whom he created artistic duets. Tragically, he died in 1988, at the age of 27.

The influence of graffiti art continues in the mass production designs of Don Ed Hardy, working with Christian Audigier. A long way from his roots as a tattooist, Hardy's work combines popular culture and marketing potential. Similar to graffiti, his images are dependent on strong pattern and line, as well as bright colorations. Many of them contain the same types of repetitive form graffiti artists have used since the 1980s.

His images are available as air fresheners, purses, fragrances, car accessories, lighters and a host of other products initially available at your local big-box store and later as items on liquidation sale at closeout stores. Mo Alabi spoke with Mr. Hardy about the experience. During the interview, Hardy said that in hindsight he realized that the agreement made his name synonymous with the 'douches' of pop culture and ultimately cheapened his personal brand. The Audigier/Hardy collaboration had made over $700 million dollars at the end of 2009.[15]

Public performances can be anything that people find entertaining, including: acrobatics, animal tricks, balloon twisting, card tricks, caricatures, clown skits, comedy, contortions, escapes, dance, singing, fire eating, fire breathing, fortune-telling, juggling, magic or mime.

Disregarding the content of their personal work, graffiti artists and street performers all address questions regarding access to public space, and as importantly, who has the right to speak in an auditory or graphic manner and what constitutes speech to begin with.

Many students are familiar with street art and are highly influenced by it in these two ways:

- Aesthetically, through strong line, color and pattern.
- Reaching out to youth directly, never engaging with the high-art gallery culture.

A culture of respect is built up around street art and tagging. Young people often know who is "real" and who is not, whose work can be painted over (or "bombed") and whose work deserves to be left alone.

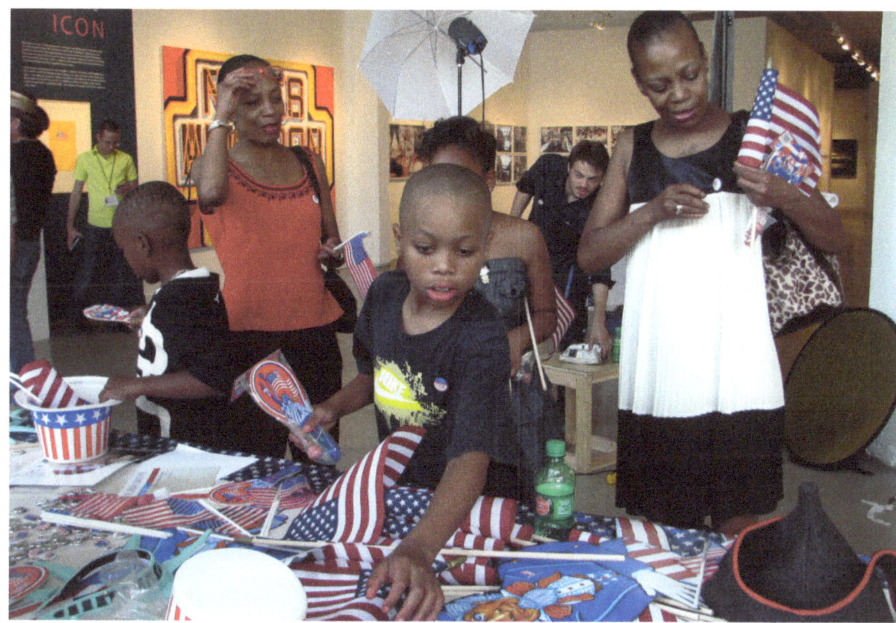

America: Now and Here, at Leedy-Voulkos Art Center, Kansas City, Missouri, 2011.

Street art practices are difficult to bring into institutional curriculum, due to the illegal nature of the process. This represents a philosophical firewall that separates street practice from traditional studio practice. Yet this style of street art speaks with clarity to many urban youth and can be a major tool in working with them.

The Hip Hop Academy, founded in Kansas City, Missouri, in 2005 by Aaron Sutton, Roscoe Johnson III and Jeremy McConnell, has been striving to bring the positive elements of hip hop art and creative culture to youth in the urban core.

Over the past several years, the Hip Hop Academy has worked with CAYD and other institutions to reach thousands of young people. Many of CAYD's social arts classes use the aesthetic language of graffiti and street performance. These techniques help engage the children, and they enjoy working with them. Organization members are keenly aware of where the legal line is drawn for assignments, keeping the students safe from arrest.

Defining Communities As Both a Relationship and an Action

A community is traditionally defined as a social group of any size whose members reside in a specific locality, share government and have a common cultural and historical heritage. In our contemporary Western technological society, communities are not simply tribes of individuals sharing the same place at the same time. Relationships to actions and issues are not merely characteristics of place, time or heritage. Rather than being static in both space and time, communities are complex relationships existing in a constant flux. They morph in and out of one another with amazing ease, as they are in constant transformation, overlapping and colliding, creating new layers of interactive relationships. Communities are not enclosures with a clear inside and outside. Boundaries and connections are important but are not frozen in time; they manifest as processes.

A group of people waiting at a bus stop form a one-dimensional group, as they are all in the act of waiting and commuting. They may be of various ages and ethnic backgrounds and work at very different jobs. The act of waiting for the bus unites them in an activity that allows for a degree of social interaction. People waiting can nod and say hello, ask each other questions, discriminate information, and under certain circumstances, even tell a joke. Communication is achieved through a non-verbalized set of rules for behavior. Riders have obtained a degree of social access to each other that they would not have simply walking down a street. If one of the commuters oversteps by breaking the unwritten rules-- becoming too personal or standing too close to someone else, making them uncomfortable--they will be shunned by the other riders.

To students of social science, the people at the bus stop may not qualify as a true community, but they provide artists both access and an opportunity to alter the one-dimensionality of this cluster of folks and to transform them into something deeper.

There are many types of potential clients for an artist to work with. Understanding the factors of group definition, how they function together, where they exist, as well as when and how they interact are all important factors. The general nature of any group of people helps to determine the artist's creative approach and outcome. Below is a list of groups to help us conceptualize possible clients and approaches for artistic action. These designations are malleable but helpful to the student or artist as they consider possibilities:

- Location: bus stops, highway information centers, construction workers eating lunch in a park, coffee shops, bars and restaurants.
- Associations and Organizations: co-workers, neighbors, sports fans, college alumni, fraternal orders, churches, political parties, street gangs, schools.
- Tradition: Christmas tree lighting ceremonies, memorial ceremonies, state fairs.
- Rituals: Burning Man, Indian pow wows, blues festivals, summer solstice celebrations, tattoo recipients, bikers.
- Issues and self-organization: environmentalism, pro-choice, pro-life, Occupy Wall Street, Tea Party.
- Physical orientation: sports, gyms, dance studios, amputee.
- Medical concerns: HIV and AIDS victims, people with diseases or conditions.
- Circumstance: auto accidents, floods, natural disasters, etc.
- Separation: wealth, race, religion.
- Culture: regional, ethnic, religious.
- Demographics: youth, age, gender, tall, short, tea drinkers.
- Technology: cell phones, computers or tablets.
- Online: gaming, message boards, news groups, social media devotees.
- Transportation: truck drivers, bikers, NASCAR fans.
- Sexuality: straight, gay, abstinence, sodomites, taboo.
- Professionals: doctors, lawyers, accountants, artists.

Date, Place, and Time

A bus stop community possible by a specific location is temporal and has very fluid boundaries. It happens at a specific place at a specific time. Where do HIV/AIDS victims or Iraqi war veterans exist in time, space or place? How would one reach them for a project? Many groups are created by having similar circumstances, such as war veterans or alumni groups They may be easily accessed in one place, such as the VFW hall. It may be possible to reach them online, through a blog or on a social networking site like Facebook or Twitter.

This form of access is much different than creating a piece intended to reach a group at a specific time and place. A Memorial Day remembrance is an example of this. A project planned for this specific day and another one planned online with a broader group of veterans would have different goals, processes and outcomes. Even within a small group, an artist should consider layers of interaction as well as access in the structural design of a project.

Projects and Approaches

There are innumerable ways to approach arts projects, but they all start with consideration of the nature of those involved and the issues they confront. Contemplation of the role of the artist and the role of others involved is the first step to successful arts actions. When artists or students begin a project, it is helpful for them to think about the following:

- History
- Issues
- Music or art
- Economics
- Culture and religion
- Place and time

Not all projects that are socially based are formed around a temporal or cohesive community. Many are formed around an issue and a self-organizing group of people who wish to participate, coming together on their own.

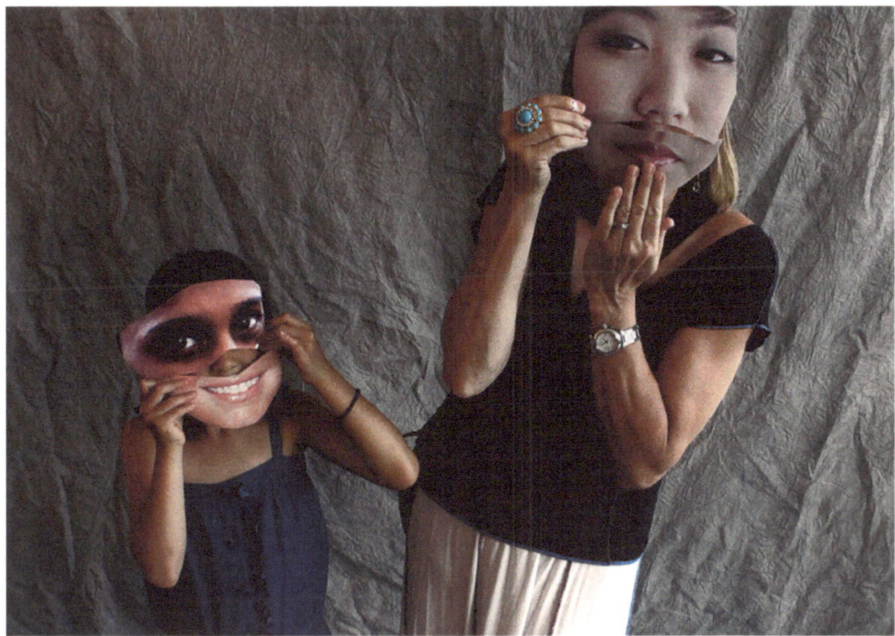

Mix Up at *America: Now and Here*, Leedy-Voulkos Art Center, Kansas City, Missouri, 2011. Photo: Emmett Merrill.

Chapter 7:
Perception and Creative Observation

Seeing the world through another person's eyes is an essential element needed to understand what makes people different from each other. Walking around in other people's shoes serves to enable a means of crossing over, so that the arts action can represent, challenge, support, and disrupt the participants as needed. The following ideas are to help artists and students move from seeing the world through their own unique lens of vision, to seeing another's narrative. This helps the artist to help others achieve their artistic voice.

Sight is not an optical event devoid of opinion and content--seeing is an intellectual act connected to personal memory, cultural awareness and value assessment. Although each person sees the world uniquely, they also have developed cultural commonalities that shape a shared vision. Tribes, clans, nations, religions and ethnic groups have characteristics that help shape a common lens that provides understanding and meaning.

While shared vision can have commonalities, an individual's perception is not limited to that singular lens. Perception is plural, and our view of the world changes as circumstances change and life progresses. A correlation between the collective lens and unique individual perception is especially of interest to the artist striving to understand how narratives develop and how an individual bridges their personal story to the story of others they are working with. It allows us to both understand stereotypes and to overcome over-simplified conceptions of people different from ourselves.

It takes informed knowledge and process to see the world through another's eyes. Creativity and skill are essential to produce and communicate a shared vision. It is a committed process to work collaboratively and express a dialogue influenced by others. Artists and students can be encouraged to consider ways that perception and creativity can be described and defined. There are many more ways of seeing than the 10 provided here as a set of guidelines for considering seeing as a process related to memory, thinking and experience.

Memory: We see what we are programmed to notice by our past experiences. When we observe something not fully understandable, we fill in the blanks often incorrectly with our memory of associated experiences. This is the process of stereotyping. In our culture, the places we grew up, our position in society and our upbringing, provide us with the memory to make automatic value judgments, both positive and negative. Our past experiences allow us to see what we are looking for. Sight is about need and desire and can often be erotic in nature. We see through attraction and elements that we desire often control our gaze.

Language: We can name the objects, moods, places and experiences we view. Language and names help us assign value to our experiences and organize our thoughts and memory. Visualization through language is pragmatic and categorical. This is the method or process for both naming and describing what we see. Words can interrupt perception. Once something is named, deeper knowledge is often curtailed as our eyes dance on to the next moment. Auditory or written descriptions give pre-conceived categorical definitions of what we notice and how we communicate these ideas to others. Naming and categorizing often hinders more insightful experiential investigation.

Intellect: Vision is inherently intellectual and biased. It is judgmental with many variables: value, outcomes, future opportunities and possible dangers. As we observe and evaluate situations we immediately see relationships and give value to the connections. What one group may value, another can see as inconsequential. Elements of import to specific people can be invisible to an outsider or even assessed as a 180 degree opposite. A positive idea for one person can be a negative idea for another.

Growing up in Alabama during the Jim Crow era, artist Hugh Merrill observed his parents' behavior when they saw an African-American man, who would have been referred to as "colored" at the time. Their opinion of the man's status was pre-determined. He was an African-American, which generated an instantaneous reaction of perceived inferiority. The cultural reasoning necessary to reach their opinion was learned prior to the moment of comprehension, so their value judgment is expressed in the simple act of recognition.

Perceived Image: Developing a view of the world through visual relations and study is a primary step in artistic progression. An individual sees the world through visual relations and forms that step outside of language and memory. An artist's view is informed; he or she sees the world as a composition. A heightened understanding of the role of form, color, lines, masses, and balance has become part of their memory, because they have been trained to see. A person with a trained eye sees the world with visual literacy, which is imperative to the artist's education.

Art education is the single most important element that differentiates the artist from people who are untrained in visual language. Their expertise is one of the important assets the artist brings to social arts practice. This knowledge and ability helps to separate the artists from other types of organizers. A social worker is not necessarily visually literate, nor is a school administrator or teacher.

Project Materials: The materials used can determine both how artists imagine a creative action and the physical qualities of the artwork. Elements used to create work are not inert. In accordance with their individual nature they demand, call for and direct marks and forms.

Pencil, paint, ink, photography, charcoal, clay or watercolor media each require changes in the way the artists sees, experiences and expresses their ideas. Artists will develop the knowledge of how to abstract the image through the materials they hold in their hand. This is also true of non-gestural processes like photography, digital media, film or video. A trained fiber artist or ceramist can see materials with an almost shamanistic pre-knowledge of forms to be created.

Aesthetics: Artists have knowledge of material, process and discipline in relationship to aesthetic form. An understanding of the core criterion that centers their discipline, coupled with historical knowledge, helps to round out their approach. This understanding forms a body of knowledge that they can change, accept or totally reject. The artist can create work that blurs traditional standards of a discipline, or they may root their work in the aesthetic heart of the discipline.

Imagination: Imagination moves beyond the perceptual and rational by altering what is expected. Perception disrupts linear thinking and categorization as well as familiar values and definitions. Similar to dreams, this inspiration allows the impossible to exist and replaces the mundane world. Developing the imagination is far from a priority in the American public school system, which is focused on teaching a set of academic skills to produce worker bees. Many students new to college have little exposure to creative problem-solving.

Compassion: Circumstances that lead to a person or group being disadvantaged should be considered before opinions about them are formed. The ability to see through the eyes of someone else and to not automatically dismiss people because they have become marginalized by the larger society is essential.

The act of serving the homeless in a soup kitchen is not enough. The ability to see the fundamental changes needed to right the injustice is a critical step. True compassion goes beyond reaching out and often accomplishes more for the one who gives the soup than the one who receives the meal. Seeing the fundamental causes of inequity is fundamental to good design. We must learn to see relationships, a map of the forces that oppress allowing a situation like homelessness to thrive.

Vision is the combination of all of the above, governed by intellect and intuition. Overall awareness is effectively rooted in the hard work of recording and creatively processing experience. Thoughts and images are conveyed to others through this cycle.

There are innumerable categories to investigate to fully understand how we see and how we interpret our realizations. The above means are meant to provide a framework for discussion.

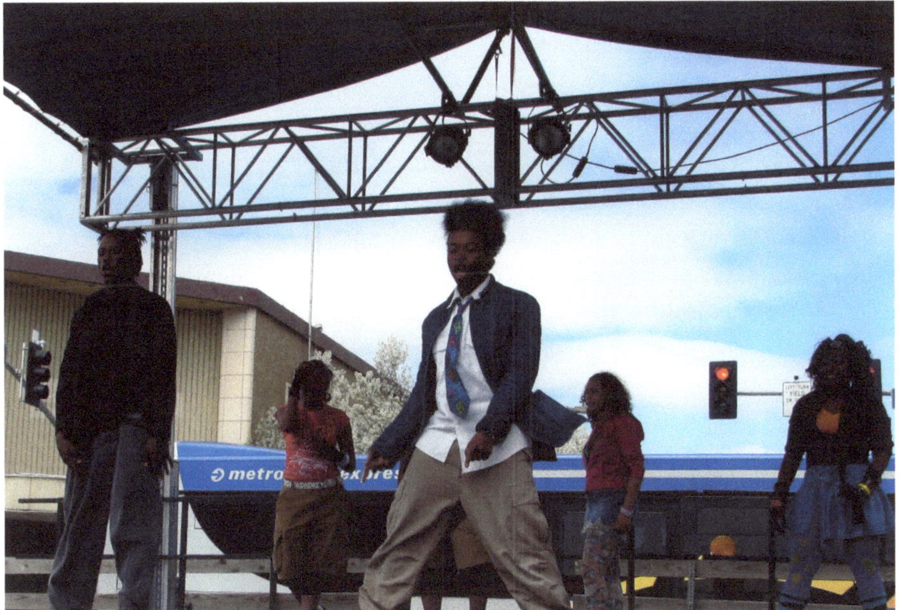

Chameleon dance group, *Happy Feet*, at the Troost Festival, Kansas City, Missouri, 2009.

Chapter 8:
Teaching Creativity

Seeing is not enough, nor is mere compassion and empathy. We need the skills to act and support communities in their creative journey. An understanding of the fundamentals of creativity will help us guide others to overcome shallow representations and help move the artistic process toward deeper discovery and understanding. All people have the ability to be creative, and all people have the ability for self-expression. The work of socially relevant artists is to provide structure and process for non-artists, creating opportunities for relevant cultural communication. Investigating creativity itself provides an important platform for future project development.

We find that creative thinking is often non-linear--insight might occur during dreaming, stepping off the curb to cross the street, or relaxing in the bath. All at once we know of an answer or correct pathway. Often, when thinking about something completely unrelated to a creative question, new ideas and solutions to the question become clear.

Can creativity be taught? Yes, absolutely. The process is similar to teaching any other thought process. Learning tools for creativity may not make a person an artist, but they can change the way a person approaches a problematic situation and help them come to a new decision.

There is a great deal written on non-linear and creative thinking; many publications describe both its importance and processes, as well as how it comes about, and how it works. In this chapter, we outline 12 concepts that are used in social arts and foundation courses at the Kansas City Art Institute to provide students with accessible tools for considering creativity. Application of these tools breaks habitual modes of approaching problems. Teachers constantly tell their students to risk and challenge themselves but seldom provide the student with a process for getting out of a predictable box.

These illustrations help the students change their habitual response to problem setting and solving. These points provide students with tools to push their ideas beyond primary considerations, to find new vantage points, produce multiple options, and restate problems. Producing multiple solutions to a single problem and re-stating the problem are both effective means of changing habitual responses.

Creative Thinking Menu: A Short List of Possibilities

Multiple Perspectives: It is important to recognize that we see the world through our own narrow experiences, habits and memories. Seeing is judgmental. Learning to step out of our own eyes and see the world through the eyes and considerations of others stimulates creativity. To think more creatively, we need to see the world from multiple perspectives. As soon as you consider or arrive at an answer to a creative problem stop and consider a new alternative solution, then a new answer, then another new answer. This is the right of first refusal. You refuse to stop your creative thinking process at the first second or third idea. Create multiple ideas and perspectives and never stop at a single idea.

Reading Cultural Inscription: Much of what we learn to say and do is determined by pressure: political, social, peer, commercial and economic. We swim in a sea of culture whose currents affect how we act. These outside forces help to make up our identity. Often we are like the ventriloquist's dummy, manipulated to act as scripted by others. Learning to read this cultural pressure and understanding how it defines us is an important step in overcoming domination and learning to speak our own minds. What are the pressures that guide our thinking in a given situation? Do we accept these pressures? Do we want to combat or emphasize these external forces? Who benefits from the cultural pressures? We need to understand the social, economic, cultural and political forces in play and design our responses and projects accordingly.

Brainstorming: Brainstorming is creative play. It is a process of seeing possibility and not conclusions. In conversation, we allow our thoughts to flow from subject to subject, unbounded and random. People involved in the dialogue do not usually take notes on what is being said.

Brainstorming can also be random, flowing from idea to idea, but all of these variations should be recorded. What is not of use today may be important tomorrow, and all ideas are opportunities. Problem solving differs from brainstorming in its focus and relationship to creating a proposed outcome. Problem solving is bounded by the need to solve a particular problem and answer the specific question asked. Extraneous ideas are limited to what is determined to be significant. Brainstorming is a process to arrive at multiple perceptions and opportunities but falls short of defining solutions. There is a natural flow between conversation, brainstorming and problem solving. One process slides easily into the next and flows back again.

When evaluating brainstorming, success

should not be measured by the solutions offered, but by the number of ideas, possibilities and opportunities presented.

Collection and Research: Creative thought is stimulated by reactions to ideas, visual material, data and information. This is why brainstorming is effective in groups. Group interaction leads to multiple perspectives and experiences being brought to bear on the problem. Research deepens thinking, yet students often rely only on their imaginations to solve visual and creative problems. An uninformed imagination will produce stereotypical answers to visual and creative questions. In socially based artistic practice, it is important that the artist goes out into the neighborhood to meet the people, as well as does academic research to inform their vision. Through collection and research, the mind is informed, and past experiences are challenged and balanced.

Non-linear Thinking: Our public school system seems dedicated to teaching to the test. They divide education into individual subjects and teach information and related skills in categorical structures. Retention of information and logic are privileged over discussion, creativity and possibility. Creativity and non-restrictive discourse are repressed by reliance on a step-by-step progression.

Non-linear thinking is thought that is differentiated by growth in multiple directions simultaneously. An oak tree grows from a single acorn, which produces a structure with roots sending nutrients up the trunk to the leaves, an organic hierarchical system. Non-linear thinking is more animated in its process than the rhizome, as thoughts jump from one topic to another. This thought process is more focused on the big picture than on the details. Non-linear thinking can throw out the stated problem and reinvent the project so that it may have little relation to the original assignment. In design and social practice, non-linear thinking is a core process, which is balanced by logic. Logic moves the investigation from brainstorming to problem and solution, which moves again to create an action plan and finally secures a conclusion. An almost complete lack of non-linear thinking practice in the American educational system leaves students with a creative thinking deficit.

The growth of bamboo is hard to control. People who know this are careful to warn others of the annoying ability of the plant to show up in seemingly impossible places. Bamboo is a perfect example of a botanical rhizome, a plant with a large root system that can create sprouts at any point. Many times these outbreaks of bamboo occur far from what appears to be the point of origin.

French psychoanalyst Felix Guattari and philosopher Gilles Deleuze developed a postmodern philosophy that explores the idea of non-heirarchical growth between random points of knowledge, based on the reproductive patterns of a botanical rhizome. As expressed in the second volume of their *Capitalism and Schizophrenia* series, *A Thousand Plateaus*, Deleuze and Guattari say: "Any point of a rhizome can be connected to anything other, and must be."[1]

Guattari and Deleuze explain their ideas through an interest in de-regulation and de-construction of energy flows, as well as matter, ideas and actions. Creative thought functions like the rhizome philosophy of growth. Artists take advantage of connections between seemingly random points, where unexpected ideas can easily occur. A de-centered network of energy can encourage artistic growth as well as organically occurring growth.[2]

In general, practicing the ability to form abstract mental connections and use non-linear thinking to envision or imagine the project is essential. This supports the development of multiple avenues of approach in considering an arts action. It is the process for listening and brainstorming with a others and drawing out several very different ideas and reactions for a project. After ideas are acknowledged, discuss them all simultaneously. This process shows respect for all contributions, and it acts as a method for arriving at the theme and structure for the final project. What may start out as a mural project with elementary school children might end as a video, in the form of a performance, projected on the exterior of the school. The video serves the same purpose that a mural would, but the media and presentation are different.

Chance Operation: Composer and artist John Cage was an early prophet of many forms of art and creativity. He said:

> *"Consider chance as an attempt to achieve something natural. Consider chance operations as a means of making a decision and how relinquishing control changes the outcome... Chance, by helping to avoid habitual modes of thinking, could in fact produce something fresher and more vital than that which the composer might have invented alone."*[3]

An artist is in the position to guide, support, and influence participants so they may see their world with greater value, cosmic comedy and insight. The artist may work to overcome negative mainstream cultural points of view, in the forms of devaluation and disregard. Chance operations integrate frequently within this mode of production.

In the early 1970s, at the Maryland Institute College of Art, Hugh Merrill had the opportunity to work with John Cage and speak with him about the creative process. Cage put a great deal of emphasis on allowing chance operations into not only the work itself, but also the thinking that occurred during the process. He clearly saw that overly engineered thinking led to predetermined outcomes, which were often shallow and unexciting. By leaving the creative process open to new opportunities provided by chance, the unexpected collisions of ideas and experiences relating to the original concept could be greatly enriched. He saw that it was not always possible to think your way to a creative outcome, but instead, acknowledged how the creation of multiple experiences brought about unexpected results which would open opportunities for further exploration and insight.

Reversal: It is easy to describe how an object could be made, but how would someone not make something? How can ideas be reversed in order to come up with a new way of approaching a problem? These questions have been fiercely contemplated historically.

A belief in the misplaced values of a society immersed in nationalist materialism contributed to the formation of Dada in 1916 by a group of Swiss literary and visual artists. They were frustrated with what they felt was an unconscious public and felt resentment and frustration over WWI, which they felt was was an unjust war. An interest in automatic writing and streaming ideas was very important to the movement, and interest in this concept continued into the work of the Abstract Expressionists. Tristan Tzara, Emily Hennings, Hugo Ball and others sought to shock society into self-awareness. Hans Arp and Hans Richter were painters involved in the movement, which moved to New York in 1915 where it caught the attention of Marcel Duchamp and Francis Picabia.[4]

These artists claimed not to be artists and insisted that their work was not to be viewed as art. Not following rules was as important as not making logical sense. Even though they viewed their work as nonsense, the Dada artists themselves were serious people with academic ideas and concerns.[5]

Marcel Duchamp's *Fountain* explains much of the viewpoint of many Dadaists. A commercially produced urinal, the piece represents a ready-made object. "Ready-made" was a term used by Duchamp to designate pieces of art chosen by an artist, as opposed to being made by the artist personally.

Dada was chosen as a nonsensical term, as the artists were not interested in anything that made sense, in a pre-determined way. The word also means various things according to different languages. Dadaists were interested in the field of discarded possibilities, asking questions like "what would never be art?" or "what defies tradition in the most extreme way?" As they started to gain the attention of the art world, they dissolved. They were angry and frustrated with the war and what they saw as the tedious mindset of larger society. They made the points they needed to make and then left, unwilling to participate in their own acceptance by society.

Tristan Tzara said "There is no Dada truth… One need only utter a statement for the opposite statement to become Dada…Dada means nothing."[6]

Imagination: As students grown, they learn to value and judge the importance of their thoughts and speech. They quickly learn to hold back their imaginative ideas, because they are afraid their peers will make fun of them. They learn to prejudge what is said and to quickly overlay new knowledge into a previously established social hierarchy. This hierarchy was passionately explored by Dadaists and Surrealists.

Revolution was what interested André Breton in the early 1920s, which is how he viewed Surrealism, the movement he founded. In direct relation to Dada, Surrealists continued Dada's interest in automatic writing and non-participation in traditional art. While centered in Paris, France, the movement quickly became global, as it resonated throughout the work of many. Some of the many participating artists include: Max Ernst, Marcel Duchamp, Joan Miro, Hans Arp, Dorothea Tanning, Louise Bourgeois and Man Ray.[7]

Influenced academically by Karl Marx and Sigmund Freud, Andre Breton wrote "Le Manifeste du Surréalisme" in 1924. He defines his ideas in this way: "Pure psychic automatism by which it is intended to express, either verbally, or in writing, the true function of thought."[8] True to Freud's musings, the unconscious was seen as the key to the purity of thought. Other writers that influenced the movement include Baudelaire, Rimbaud and Lautréamont. Rimbaud was seen as completely indifferent to the importance of his own work, making him appear as a human automaton, a subject of interest at the time.[9]

Surrealist artists were interested specifically in the effects of dreams on reality, which caused them to be wary of the validity of conscious thought. Their explorations into violence, sexuality and decay gave their work a raw quality both visually and viscerally. This was seen as a means to purity of expression. They had given a voice to the human qualities of hunger, anger, shame, anxiety and hopelessness. They sought to move beyond the mundane, in the form of everyday conscious thought, strongly convinced there was more to the mind that what we could think of while awake. The thoughts of children were seen as purer than those of adults, as adults had repressed their thoughts through consciousness.[10]

It is helpful to concentrate on suspending disbelief and beliefs. A child's imagination is a stream of ideas and images, which often disregards rationality. Children learn to play; adults learn to solve problems. Learning to combine the imaginative play of the child and the problem-solving qualities of an adult is hard work.

Reading the history of an object and deductive reasoning: Sherlock Holmes used his powers of deductive reasoning to solve fictional crimes. He filled the gaps between clues by reading their hidden story. Deduction is the ability to look at objects and imagine their history based on visual clues. Deduction is informed imagination. It allows imagination to move beyond labeling, to understanding past functions and origin. Deduction is also a method of critical evaluation in considering the quality of design, function and aesthetic value of an object.

Collaboration: Most of our work in school, especially art school, is evaluated on individual achievement, authorship and a uniqueness of vision. Much professional creative work is collaborative. The disciplines of design, film, animation, music, and socially relevant art are collaborative intersections between groups: clients, artists, designers, technicians, and communities.

Simply throwing a group together to do a project will not necessarily lead to good collaborative practice. Collaboration has to be taught. In order to collaborate, you must learn to be open and share. Learn to listen, and stimulate the imagination and voice of the people contributing with you. Too often, collaboration is taken for granted, but it is a complex social interaction marked by ego and narrow understanding of outcome. Much of what our society and culture have taught us in western society is that the lone individual voice is the one to be highly regarded. Learning to turn off these deeply embedded systems of thought are difficult, to say the least. The student should progress through a series of experiences that counter learned habits of individualized thought and production.

The land of Not and the land of Is: A correct and habitual answer is what can be thought of as the land of is. It is a stereotypical right answer. "What is a soccer ball?" We all know the answer to the question. A soccer ball is a specific object. Everything else that is not a soccer ball lives in the land of not, simply because it is not a soccer ball. Interestingly, when children want to play soccer and there is no soccer ball available, that does not stop them. Almost anything can become the ball: an empty can, ball of rags, a tennis ball, or an empty bleach container. The creative answer most often is in the land of not instead of the land of is. Asking students what they would not do to solve a problem can serve to open the field of discarded possibilities.

Language: Language can be a barrier to creativity. To name something categorizes its function and place in the world. Language is a concept for a real thing or action and not the thing itself. We may know what a ball is and be able to recognize and describe it in scientific terms. To really know what a ball is, you have to kick it, catch it, throw it and so on. A kiss is even a better example. To be able to name something is not the same as knowing it.

To see something in a new way, the automatic acceptance of a literary description or definition is not enough. Learning to rephrase and restate questions or descriptions, while considering new ways of defining and thinking about the action or object, is what makes it meaningful.

One Artist's Creative Thought Process

Artist Eric Fischl's description of how he created the painting *Bad Boy* provides a journey inside the creative thinking process.[11] In his lecture at the Nelson-Atkins Museum of Art in Kansas City, Missouri, in the spring of 2011, Fischl described this process. He started with a large canvas and originally wanted to paint a still life of a bowl and fruit. He painted the still life in the lower left section of the canvas.

Then he asked himself, "What would the still life be sitting on?" He decided it would be a dresser rather than a table. If it was a dresser, it would be in a bedroom, and if it was in a bedroom, he determined that he should paint a bed.

On the bed he painted a nude woman. He then asked himself, "What is she doing?" He painted an infant sleeping next to her. Then he painted the baby nursing. He did not respond well to the baby, so he removed the child and painted a young boy with his hand behind his back, standing at the end of the bed staring at the sleeping nude woman. He asked himself, "Why does the boy have his hand behind his back?" It was at that moment when he realized the boy had entered the room to steal money from the woman's pocket book.

Many, if not most, viewers will assume Fischl had the completed image in his mind and painted it directly, as if he were looking at a photograph of the image in his mind. In reality, the work comes from a creative dialogue and intuitive storytelling process. Fischl had all the skill needed to paint the image itself, but technical skill alone did not allow him to arrive at the final work. The process could be described as non-linear thinking, or daydreaming, instead of high-level logical and analytical thought.

There is also a level of chance in the process; as Fischl painted *Bad Boy*, it became what his imagination dreamed of. His imagination informed him with new possibilities on a daily, if not hourly, level.

Fischl's process includes trying one idea then disregarding it to try another. Each decision opens new pathways to explore the next, which is unknown or unimagined until the process progresses to where new options suddenly become relevant. Fischl realized that the process

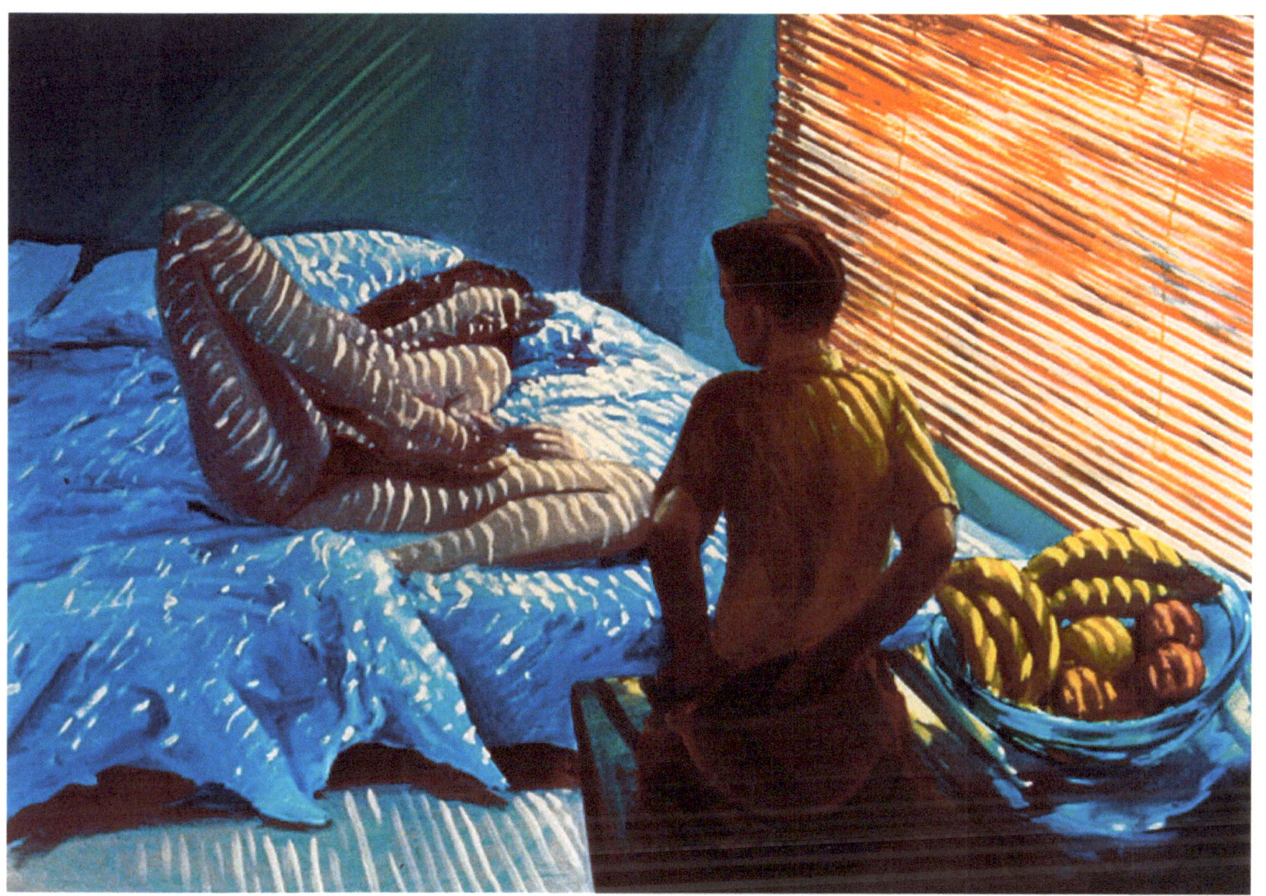

Eric Fischl, *Bad Boy*, oil on canvas, 66' x 96'. ©Eric Fischl.

of decisions, changes, and new possibilities will lead to the final poetic image. He trusted in both his skills as a painter and as a creative intellectual.

Creative thinking is difficult to define. We know the painting *Bad Boy* was created using specific methods of context and process to move the work forward. In more academic terms, creativity is interconnected with other forms of higher thinking: logic, conception, insight, divergent, and convergent thinking.

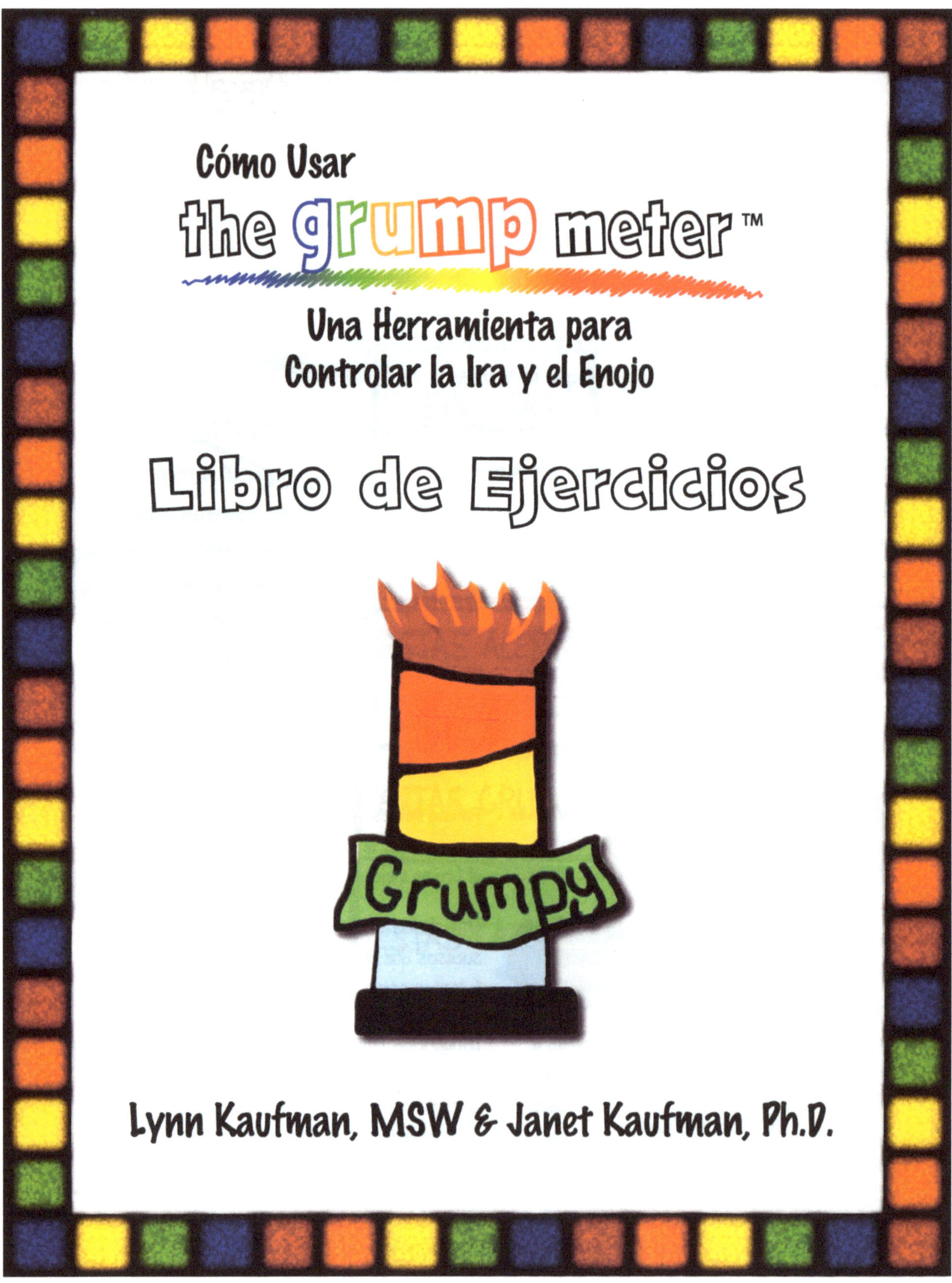

Cómo Usar
the grump meter ™
Una Herramienta para
Controlar la Ira y el Enojo
Libro de Ejercicios
Grumpy
Lynn Kaufman, MSW & Janet Kaufman, Ph.D.

Insights From A Supposed Art Teacher:
The Emmanuel's Community Center Book Project

Facilitated by Lauren McGill

Lauren McGill and Chameleon Arts, *Insights from a Supposed Art Teacher: Emmanuel's Community Center Book Project*, Kansas City, Missouri, 2013 - 2015.

Opposite page: Janet Kauffman, Lynn Kauffman and Chameleon Arts, *The Grump Meter*, a youth-at-risk anger control and portrait project in conjunction with Surel's Place Arts Residency, Boise, Idaho, 2016.

Chapter 9:
Assignments

These assignments are meant to provide the student with fundamentals for creative thinking. The focus of these exercises is simply to get the student to consider how they think, perceive and interface with reality. After they hone their abilities they can then use their new tools to challenge habits of thinking to see what else they might come up with. As community-based artists, they will lead brainstorming sessions to encourage community members to participate in a dialogue. These tools will allow them to both listen more intently and better help the community to articulate and challenge their own habits and assumptions. If applied well, these exercises can help a community of non-artists delve deeper into their concerns, ideas and conceptions about a project or issue.

These descriptions and insights, written by Hugh Merrill, take a step-by-step approach to each exercise. They are suitable for a range of ages and demographics, and educators are encouraged to personalize these ideas and keep in touch with him about the results they have seen.

Assignment #1:

Draw a birdhouse

This exercise teaches that the correct answer is seldom the creative and innovative answer. The group is first asked to draw a birdhouse. I have done this exercise with social workers, grad students, art students at all levels and from all disciplinary backgrounds. Inevitably the students draw a simple birdhouse with a hole for a door and a perch. Most of the class will draw the standard birdhouse with a slanted roof, a hole for the door and a peg for the bird to sit on. Someone usually draws a nest in a tree. I have asked what led them to think of a nest in the tree instead of a birdhouse. A typical response is that they thought of the birdhouse first, then the tree, and then elected to draw the tree. This is the right of first refusal, which is a door to the creative process. By refusing to use the first answer, even though you know it is correct, you open up to alternative possibilities. Going from the first answer, to ask for a second, third or fourth response forces the person to continue to think about and redefine the question. This is the first step in basic strategies for creative thinking.

First refusal means not accepting your first answer even if you think it is correct. Going beyond the habit of stopping the investigation or thinking process, simply because you have the right answer, is what prevents new ideas. In fact, the moment you have the correct answer, it is time to immediately ask "What else is a birdhouse?" or "What else could it be?"

For many years at the Kansas City Art Institute, the sculpture department gave elective students the assignment of building a birdhouse. The class became a woodshop project with the students constructing elaborate birdhouses: split levels, castles, and Frank Lloyd Wright influenced structures. One student built this: he dug holes and cemented four 4' x 4' ten-foot-tall posts into the ground, creating the outline of a rectangle. Then he built a platform eight feet off the ground and added a ladder so he could climb onto the platform and drill holes in the upper section of the 4' x 4' posts to insert tree limbs to act as perches.

Later, he placed a large bale of hay on the platform and buried two galvanized buckets in the hay, one with bird food and one with water. The contraption was situated in a field on campus near a line of old trees. While no birds cared to move into the other well-crafted birdhouses, hundreds of fowl flocked to this one. They built nests in the near by trees with the straw from the bail of hay and had a continuous supply of birdseed and water. After about a week, the lower portion of the campus felt like the Hitchcock movie *The Birds*, and the mess they had made led to the school asking that the piece be removed, which the artist did with a smile.

The young man who facilitated this habitat was Russell Ferguson, who is now the chair of the Foundation Department at the Kansas City Art Institute. I asked Russell how he came up with the idea. He (like almost everyone else) thought of the standard birdhouse and put that idea aside. Other architectural alternatives came to mind, which he also rejected. Once out of the spell of an architectural answer, he thought a tree was the best environment for birds. So how do you build a better tree? The answer to this question is to create a situation where safety, food, water and nesting material all come together, so the combination of elements can form an ecosystem for the birds.

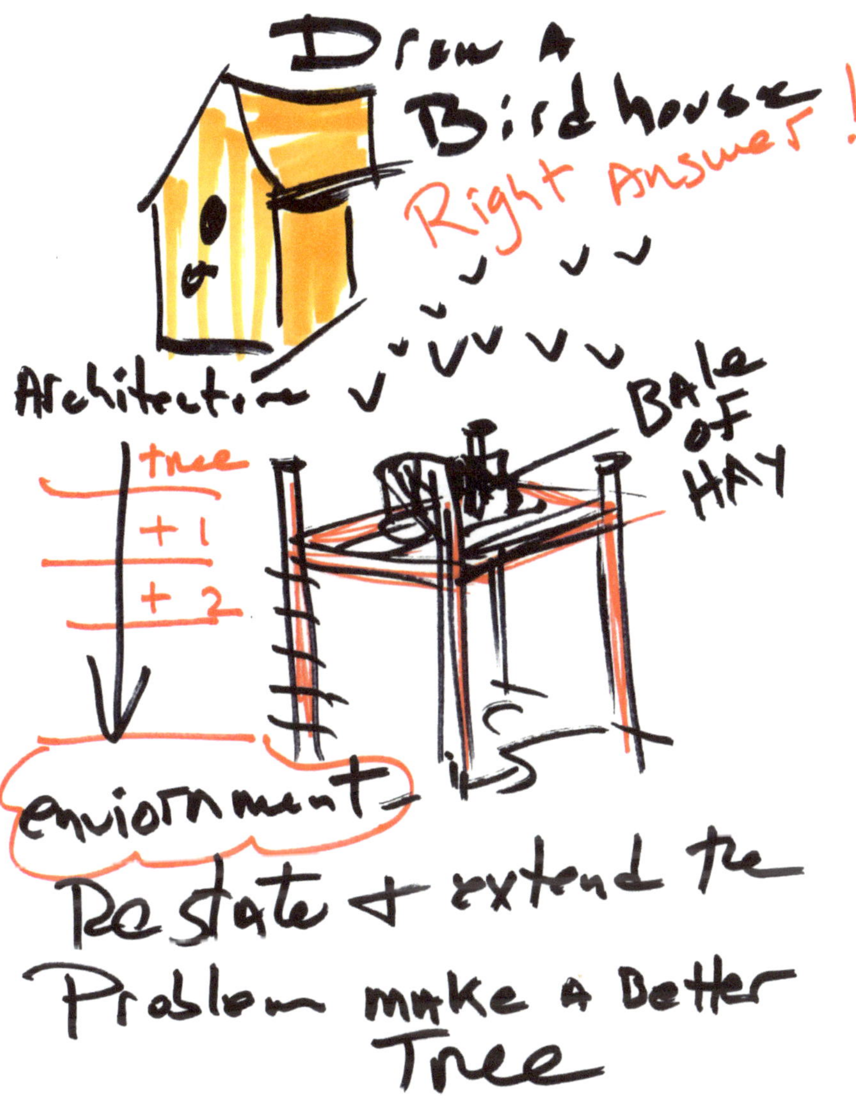

Whiteboard drawing of *Draw a Birdhouse*, 2013.

The exercise reinforces the following strategies:

- Right of first refusal, do not act on your first and correct answer.

- Do not stop with a single answer. Always come up with multiple solutions to exercises.

- Brainstorm.

- Capture and create multiple ideas rather than problem solve.

- Expand and restate the problem from "Draw a birdhouse" to "Reinterpret what a birdhouse is" or "What makes a better birdhouse?"

- To effectively extend the scope of investigation, change the language of the question.

Assignment #2:
Reversal: The Land of Not is Greater Than the Land of Is.

We often think we know what something is, and we certainly seem to know what something is not. We know what a birdhouse is and that a pumpkin is in a different category. Or is it? The creative solution to many questions is not to be found in their definitions. In the land of is, the more creative and valuable answer is found in the land of not.

In a sense, we change directions and reverse the problem. When students are asked to draw a birdhouse, they are first being asked what a birdhouse is. Before an object can be drawn, what it is should be established. If we reverse the question, we concentrate on what the object is not. This significantly opens the field of opportunity and possibility. Yes, a pumpkin can definitely be a birdhouse.

We all know a self-portrait when we see one. Usually, it takes the form of a face painted, drawn, photographed, sculpted or carved. A more interesting question is, "What is not a self-portrait?" Change the question slightly, to "How would you not make a self-portrait?" These new questions provide much more interesting creative opportunities.

Assignment #3:
What Would You Not Do to a Sheet of Paper?

I ask the class to write down what they would not do to a sheet of paper and let them know they have about two minutes to perform the task. I then ask them how many students have 10 answers, then 9, 8, 7, 6, 5, 4, and then down to zero. One or two people will have more than a single answer, and several will have zero. I point out that the form of the question did not ask for a single answer, and again (like the birdhouse assignment) the singular response is a starting point for continued consideration.

Creativity is based on multiple possibilities and not single answers. The American public school system is not built on discussion and creative thinking. It is built on answering questions on standardized tests that rank achievement. The answers become important in relation to the outcome of the test only, not the deeper intellectual discourse they may foster. Art schools work to reverse the knee-jerk habits of single, simple answers, attributing one right answer to each question only. A correct answer often blocks more interesting alternatives.

I have the students read their answer(s), and they sound like this:

- *I would not eat a piece of paper.*
- *I would not build a house out of paper.*
- *I did not answer the question, because there is nothing I would not do with paper.*
- *It was a stupid question, so I did not answer.*

We examine the answers and discover several processes of thinking that block creative thinking and participation. As soon as a reaction is written down, the person questions whether or not the answer is true. Answers are analyzed either with "accept" or "reject." The ability to suspend belief has been lost. As John Cage says: "You cannot make and analyze at the same time." Creating a number of possibilities prior to shifting to analytical thinking is crucial. When I ask young children a question, they spout many retorts, because they are seldom blocked by truth, reality, or fear of failure.

Typical answers from children include: "I would not make a dragon, or an airplane, or shoes." They automatically give multiple answers, and they laugh and enjoy the question. Children

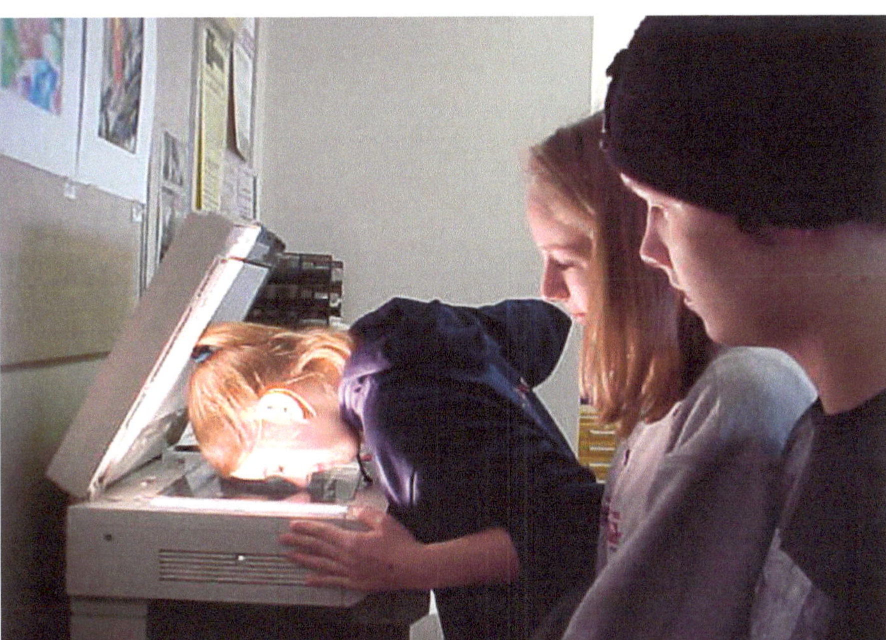

Portrait assignment at the Kansas City Art Institute, 2013.

have not forgotten how to play and imagine. Adults worry about how they will be perceived or how their classmates will react to them if the question turns out to be a joke. They are nervous about being taunted by classmates. Feeling awkward and embarrassed causes a disconnection in process and participation. They make a predetermination of what a stupid question this is, so they can try to position themselves above answering it. Typically, they are wary that they are being tricked.

Adults have a fear of being wrong. School has reinforced the attitude that it is better not to participate than to be in error. Test scores and social judgments arc both affected by incorrect responses, leading many to opt out if they can.

The form of the question takes the student into the vast creative space of the land of not. "What would you do to a piece of paper" only reinforces the obvious. "What you would not do to a piece of paper" is infinite and always creative, contradictory and surreal. The question opens up the imagination to stimulate silly, visionary and fantastically impossible responses.

Assignment #4:
Or: Multiple Perspectives

Or is a simple game where the student states an idea or problem for their creative work and is then asked by the rest of the class, "Or?" They have to quickly come up with a second, third and fourth variation of the idea. Quick thinking is important to the process. At this stage, it is important to deny them time to think or ponder an answer to the question. The variation must come quickly from their imagination, without time for judgment.

The process can then be reversed, which allows students time to research their in-class responses. They can then come to the next class with ten new ideas inspired from the first section. Research material that has informed their new search, such as library books, web sites, or internet searches is brought in for review. The goal is to teach the student to use quick and unfiltered imagination, coupled with a deeper process of research. Both fast and slow are important tools.

Detailed research should be incorporated into the journey, reaching beyond a personal limited scope of knowledge, and toward a broader cultural foundation. Invariably, the student's first idea is disregarded for one of the new variations.

Here is an example of what a student, Becky, said while working through this problem:

I want to make a self-portrait, or?

- A drawing of myself (pause) in a mirror, or?
- A photo of myself, or?
- A picture of myself driving away in a car, or?
- A landscape, or?
- A picture of myself as a landscape, in a landscape, or?
- I will use family photos of myself as a child, because we lived on a farm, and I will do a drawing, or?

Later in the conversation, Becky expressed she would make all of these things and put them in one work. She then lost enthusiasm and shouted "no more, no more!" She laughed and the class chanted "or, or, or."

Becky's final project was a folded journal that could be unfolded and shown on a gallery wall. It was a combination of written memories of her childhood and weekly drawings of herself.

Assignment #5:
Deduction

This exercise can be done with any set of objects. I started using chairs because in the printmaking studio at the Kansas City Art Institute there are a very odd and eclectic bunch of chairs. Over the years, the school has bought different metal chairs, some dating back to the 1970s and some from the last couple of years. The students have brought in chairs of every description. Most of them were found sitting by the side of the road– they were picked up and eventually brought to the school. There are dining room chairs, rolling desk chairs, a variety of folding chairs, and an occasional living room lounge chair. The one thing they all have in common is they have been well used as well as misused. I select three from this group and place them on a worktable. The students are then asked to tell stories relating to the furniture. At first, they do not have a clue or they are guarded and slow to respond, so I prompt them with these questions:

- *What was the original value of the different chairs?*
- *What were they originally designed for?*
- *What does the design of the objects have to do with their function?*
- *Who were they designed for?*
- *Who were their original owners?*

As the students warm up, they begin to consider the materials, design, and craftsmanship of the pieces. They imagine the rooms that they would have originally been placed in, and who might have owned them. What were their owners like? How much money did they make and where did they work? Then they consider what caused the wear and tear on the chairs. Children, pets, age and everyday use are all relevant.

Developing the ability to look at the story behind each object or place, to see the story that is being told, helps to hone creative thought. The students are then asked to make a graphic drawing to tell each chair's individual story.

Chance Operation

The roots of using chance operations to generate visual art and poetry can be traced back to the Dada movement in the early twentieth century, as briefly discussed in the previous section on creativity and non-linear thinking. The Dadaists believed that the mind would create associations and meaning from any text, including those generated through random selections. In one section of Tzara's *Dada Manifesto on Feeble & Bitter Love*, he offers the following instructions to make a Dadaist poem, here translated from the original French by Barbara Wright:

> *Take a newspaper.*
> *Take some scissors.*
> *Choose from this paper an article the length you want to make your poem.*
> *Cut out the article.*
> *Next carefully cut out each of the words that make up this article and put them all in a bag.*
> *Shake gently.*
> *Next take out each cutting one after the other.*
> *Copy conscientiously in the order in which they were chosen from the bag.*
> *The poem will resemble you.*
> *And there you are–an infinitely original author of charming sensibility, even though unappreciated by the vulgar herd.*[1]

I was fortunate to meet many artists that would achieve the status of icons as both an undergraduate and a graduate student. When I attended the Maryland Institute College of Art, an artist from New York named Emanuel Navaretta would come down and teach class once a week. Sometimes he brought John Cage and Allen Ginsberg down to hang out.

Navaretta, Ginsberg and Cage came to my studio to look at my work. As we sat and talked, I got up the nerve to show Ginsberg my poetry. He took my notebook and read through a rather long poem I had written. He sat quietly. When he finished thinking, he then handed me the notebook and said with a smile, "Paint." Cage and Navaretta laughed in a good-hearted way. It was perhaps the best and most truthful critique I would ever have. Cage then told me to try making a game of writing, find a way to get in and beyond myself.

On the table was a spinner from a children's game, the kind with an arrow you can spin, which stops on different colored triangles that form a circle with numbers in sections of a pie-shaped game board. Earlier, Cage had picked up the spinner and asked me what I knew about, in general terms. He also asked what subjects I liked. I said "Family, Civil War stuff, girlfriends, hanging out in the Mt. Royal Tavern and pets." He interrupted and then suggested I write down a symbol for each subject on the spinner, using the numbers ranging from one to six on the board to symbolize minutes. "Take it for a spin," he said. "Once to find the subject, and then a second time to find the number of minutes you will write about it.

His advice to me was to open my mind to the chance interaction of time and subject, based on my interest, to help to engage and disrupt my thinking. I took Cage's advice, but I have no doubt that Ginsberg was correct: I should stick to visual language. The experience had a positive impact on my prints to this day. I continue to mix content and preconceived design with chance visual operations to free the work from my own habits and control.

Describe a Hidden Object

If I give a class the assignment to draw an eye, they all know the visual symbol commonly used to represent it. They are also in agreement about the symbol for an ear. When they are asked what a visual symbol for the middle of the back would look like, they find this is not an easy depiction. Symbols act much like words, and symbols in themselves are a bridge between visual and word-based language. To help the students go beyond words and definitions, try describing simple objects, and then ask the students to draw the qualities of the descriptions, rather than the object itself. Drawings produced in this way are often quite remarkable and have little resemblance to the object being described. This project reinforces moving beyond the simple language-based definitive responses seen in the birdhouse problem.

Draw these qualities based on a description of an object. When you finish, do you then know what the object is? Could you have guessed and drawn the object from these terms?

1. Multiple layers
2. Lamination
3. Oval shape
4. Grid pattern
5. Wrapping
6. Tensile strength
7. Handle
8. Curves

(The answer is a tennis racket.)

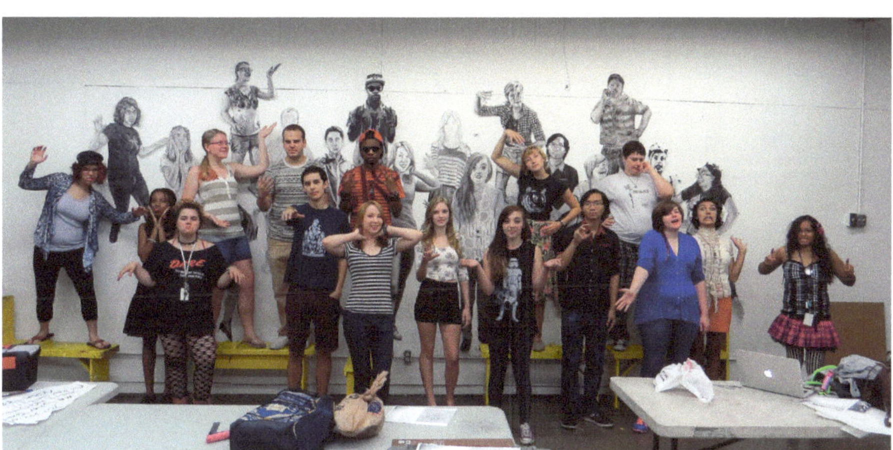

Youth community portrait project, Kansas City Art Institute, 2013.

Brainstorming and Collaboration

Great groups have shaped our world, from the gathering of young geniuses at Los Alamos who unleashed the atom, to the youthful scientists and hackers who invented a computer that was personal as well as powerful. That should hardly surprise us. In a society as complex and technologically sophisticated as ours, the most urgent projects require the coordinated contributions of many talented people . . . And yet, even as we make the case for collaboration, we resist the idea of collective creativity. Our mythology refuses to catch up with our reality. And so we cling to the myth of the Lone Ranger, the romantic idea that great things are usually accomplished by a larger-than-life individual working alone.[2]

There are many threads that come together in educating artists and designers, including: skill, history, popular culture, innovation, discipline-based perspectives, aesthetics and creative thinking. These various threads come to fruition in the artist/student's individual studio narrative, integrating authorship of ideas with development of art objects.

Collaboration is often a hidden concern, if it is considered at all, in many studio visual arts programs. Studio-based education can be broken down into a progression of four steps:

- Concept/motivation
- Production/technique
- Evaluation/remaking
- Interpretation/critique

Work is often done in a lab or studio where students can view each other's work and interact with it. Informal discussion is built into the architecture of the studio space or classroom. The process and the studio space are accommodating to working together, but the main emphasis is usually on individual growth and authorship. Final evaluation and assessment is firmly based on the individuals perceived intellect and creativity. The traditional progression of the history of contemporary art and art history in general is firmly based in one set of ideas jumping over the next, driven by individual genius artists. There are fundamental qualities to this system that will, and should remain, as art always moves into the future. Individual vision will eventually be equally balanced by collaborative projects, as more and more young artists move their work in this direction. One-hundred years from now, rather than individuals driving the story of art, it may well be that the story will be told through community and collaborative actions.

We are living in a swiftly changing paradigm in which relationships outpace individualism. The act of buying a plastic bottle of water from the local convenience store has moral and environmental consequences. Unbounded individual freedom, celebrated for more than two centuries, is being replaced by a connective, collaborative and complex series of mutual relationships. Each artist's act, like buying the water bottle, is connected to the whole, and the eventual value will be judged on the outcome of the web of relationship they engender and not as an avant-garde act of individual discoveries in specialized disciplines.

In fact, the art world has moved far beyond disciplinary categories, such as painting, to interdisciplinary practices that not only combine artistic disciplines but also call for collaboration with science, psychology, social work, urban planning and many others areas of action. Visual arts education is struggling to reinvent itself in light of interdisciplinary practice, relational aesthetics and new technologies.

The application of the artist's vision will no longer be a progression from classroom or studio to gallery representation and the hope of eventual celebrity status. The artist will function in a broader world of relationships and responsibilities that necessitates collaboration with others. Visual creativity has already expanded the audience of participants from gallery goers to micro communities. Artists will continue to challenge other non-arts disciplines to utilize artistic processes and actions to change the real world problems they are dealing with.

An interconnected ensemble of voices will not simply replace the individual in their studio, but over the next decade, the mythology of the lone wolf artist will be eclipsed. This group dynamic is to be expected in a shrinking world that is highly interconnected, complex and increasingly technologically sophisticated. The most compelling projects will require the coordination of varied disciplines, diverse communities, and the involvement of multiple interdisciplinary originators.

This is how art moves forward in history, as the brilliant expression of the gifted individual becomes a collaborative voice of multiple participants.

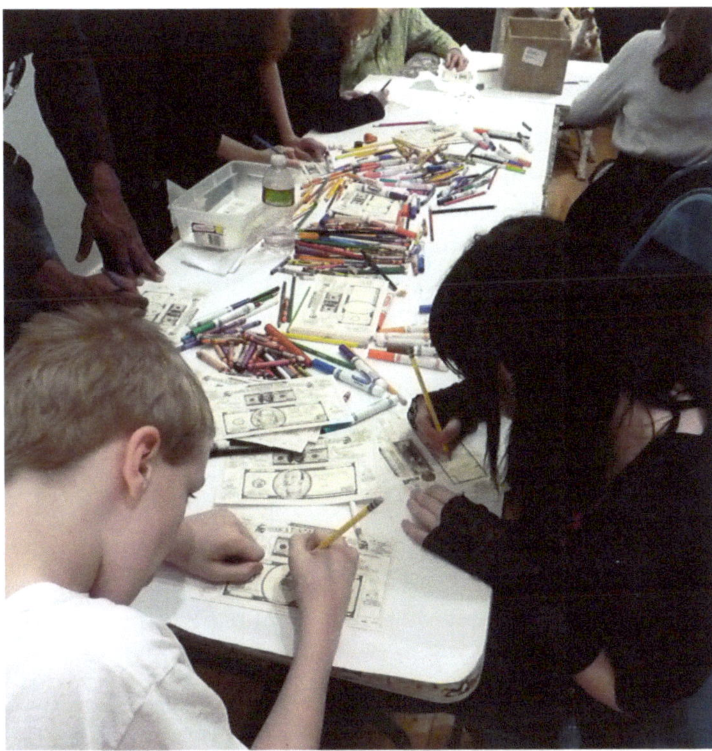

Drawing Fundred $100.00 bills, Mel Chin's *Fundred Dollar Bill Project*, Kansas City, Missouri, 2010.

Chapter 10
Teaching Collaborative Assignments and Discussion

When students were asked to collaborate on projects in the mid-late 1990s, the students worked sequentially but not collaboratively. They did not know how to create effective group discussion or how to value the ideas and thoughts of others. With little or no knowledge of how to challenge or assess ideas and foster discussion they often ended with poor working relations within the group. People who naturally took the lead overpowered quieter individuals, and creative opportunities were missed. There was a split between leaders and worker bees that were asked to do more humble activities, while the leaders took the more intellectual, creative, and administrative roles.

Collaboration is not simply a matter of assigning the problem and expecting the students to know how to work together.

One example of this was illustrated by asking groups of three students to produce a 4' x 8' woodblock print. Rather than discussing, dreaming or designing together, each student would take turns producing an initial drawing or carving the woodblock. They avoided discussion of the possible theme or the hard work of critically designing the image based on a collaborative and conceptual vision. It was easier for them to say something such as, "Let's have everyone do what they want and see what happens." They knew enough about their own working process and creativity to reject being tied down to a system, and none of them wanted to be the worker bees for someone else's design. They all wanted to be free to express and react without restraint. Finally, and as importantly, they did not feel comfortable in criticizing someone's idea or contribution.

Creation of a collaborative drawing, print or sculpture allowed the students to respond in an informal and sequential process of making. The outcome was often a remarkable but dysfunctional work, so the energy level of the students always carried the day. This process did not achieve a level of collaborative interaction that would allow the students to work together effectively on a project, and the possibility of making effective art projects with a non-arts people would have been out of the question for them.

A simple lecture about collaboration would not suffice in helping the students make the most of group creative practice. They needed to start at the root of collaboration by first defining it and then discovering how to best approach working together in a group, as opposed to individually working next to each other.

Collaboration is by nature discursive and based on conversation, listening and learning to help folks articulate their ideas and thoughts. During the process of creating ideas, everything expressed should be documented, no matter how far off the mark it may seem at the time. Investigation of the collaborative process can begin by examining the process of discussion. In this chapter, we attempt to define the differences between conversation, discussion, brainstorming and problem solving. Each level of communication is similar, yet has differing outcomes and structures. Over the years, students and instructors have come up with these rough divisions:

Conversation: Conversation is marked by a casual nature and can be easily interrupted and the direction instantly changed. At any point, subjects may return or veer off in completely unexpected directions. For example: A group of students are sitting in a coffee shop and seriously discussing the existence of God, the end of war, or some other weighty issue, when a friend walks in and the table erupts in high-fives and invitations to join the group. After this point the theme shifts and never returns to the issue of war or God but veers off to last night's adventures, friends, or gossip. Conversation is usually not recorded, and efforts to capture it are few and far between. Talk is free-flowing, but can be very serious and insightful. The emergence of conversational ideas becomes something original and engaging.

Discussion: The students in the coffeeshop were discussing war and God. Discussion is more systematic and focused than free-flowing conversation. It can be part of a private exchange or take place in a structured public event. Discussion is topical and attempts to penetrate an issue or theme as a means of trying to explain or establish a point of view. An exchange of views can be political in nature, expressing a point of view and convincing others of the validity of that point of view. It is a process of theoretical and speculative debate that can lead to developing hypothetical models, particularly about religion, politics and culture.

Discussions are often held in school to allow the students to think and consider an issue from multiple points of view, to voice differing opinions and to test the students' understanding of ideas. The ability to articulate these skills is fundamental for panel presentations at academic conferences or business meetings. Discussion is fundamental to knowledge, as it is a process of stating a belief

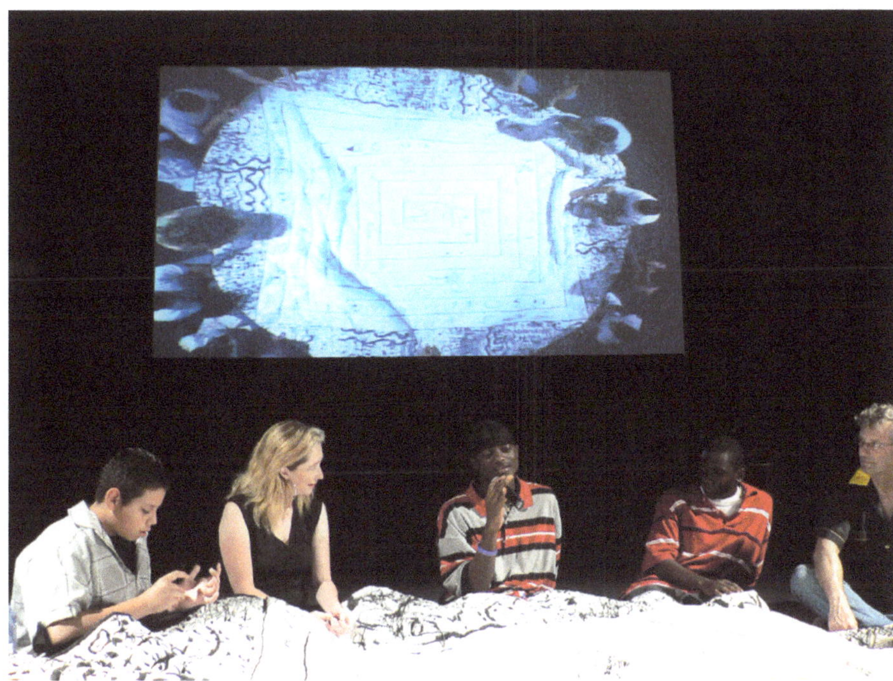

So Yeon Park, *Storytelling and Listening*, presented at the YWCA in Kansas City, Kansas, 2009.

and simultaneously evaluating that belief. Often there are two sides or points of view competing for acceptance. Capture ideas and the points being discussed so that they can be supported or rejected.

Brainstorming: A problem or situation is at the root of the collaborative process. Brainstorming begins when something needs to be investigated, changed, or created. A group comes together with the goal of considering a problem and coming up with multiple options. Brainstorming is highly creative and calls for thinking beyond ordinary personal investigation. If an individual could easily address the question, there would be no need for a group to attempt to come up with new points of view. Brainstorming can be effective for an individual, but is most often a group activity, searching for multiple courses of action.

Brainstorming is free-flowing like conversation and directed like discussion. Unlike casual conversation, where ideas and thoughts float away into the air, brainstorming demands that the thoughts are recorded and later assessed to determine their validity and potential for future application. Although brainstorming is directed at a problem, condition, or topic, the process is inherently non-linear in nature. All opportunities are valid but some will turn out to be better for the present situation than others. The relevant ideas will be built on later to further advance the investigation of solving the problem. The tangential ideas, though not of use at the present, are still possibilities for new searches or future considerations and need to be recorded and respected.

Problem solving: Problem solving is based on the evaluation and assessment of ideas that have bubbled up during brainstorming. It is moving from a broad vision to a question that is clearly articulated. The broad vision stated during the brainstorming is now open to the questions of "How will we do this?" or "How will we create and develop this idea?" Brainstorming provides multiple facets of an idea and multiple articulations of the problem.

Problem solving is a clearer statement of what can be achieved, a narrowing of opportunities to a manageable and clear direction of investigation, starting with an organizational activity which breaks the problem down into smaller parts. It is not only a conceptual activity, but instead, involves materials and attempts to bring the activity to fruition. Adapting the conceptual prototype to real world consequences, such as funding and budgets, access to materials and other real world conditions impacts the realization of the vision.

Working together builds involvement that is beneficial in producing coordinated actions that overcome obstacles to bring the project nearer to fruition. These common difficulties occur frequently:

- Students are resistant to limiting themselves and others.
- Students are unable to effectively work within specific themes or parameters.
- Some may feel uncomfortable criticizing the contributions of others.
- There are difficulties in scheduling times for all members of the group to work together.
- Some students may want to work alone on the project.
- Some have poor listening skills and talk over others.
- Some students are overly judgmental of ideas and remarks.

A New Game of Chess

After an open discussion of collaboration, brainstorming, conversation and problem solving, I take a survey of the students and ask questions such as "What is your major?" or "What skills do you have?" I ask them to include skills beyond the visual arts, such as leadership, communication, singing, playing an instrument or math. Non-arts skills are as important as any specific art skill they possess.

I list their names and skills on a dry erase board. After they finish this portion of the class, I ask them to divide themselves into groups based solely on a distribution of skills. Once the groups are formed, I ask them to re-invent the game of chess. About half of them moan and say they know little about chess, while others become excited. I tell them they will often have to collaborate and work on problems that are beyond their comfort zone. They are reminded that the worst people to re-invent the game would be grand master players who seemingly know every aspect there is to know.

What they come up with is always interesting and diverse, but the actual outcomes are not the point of the exercise. The real goal is to introduce students to the basic skills required for collaboration and brainstorming. The first time they collaborate with their group, the following is likely to occur and needs correction:

- One or two people take over the brainstorming session and direct the discussion toward their idea.
- A single detailed outcome becomes the main point of emphasis.
- People who are naturally quiet provide little input to the discussion.
- Students do not keep accurate notes or visuals.
- The session is more like conversation than brainstorming, and little of the discussion is captured.
- The conversation moves too quickly to problem solving.
- Students may only be concerned with discovering a right answer that they think is expected from them.
- Students choose to engage in attempts to be clever and do not effectively participate. For example, they may say chess is the perfect game and cannot be reinvented.

I interrupt them after 15 minutes and ask them to show me their process and to explain how they are thinking about the problem. They usually do not answer that question, but instead tell me about the outcome – an example might be: "We invented chess played with live players in a field." After each group has spoken, I take them back to the beginning of the conversation and discuss the importance of collaborative process. "Why did you come up with only a single answer and go so into detail so fast?" or "Why are there no notes or drawings to support your idea?" I emphasize that producing a single answer is not a desired outcome

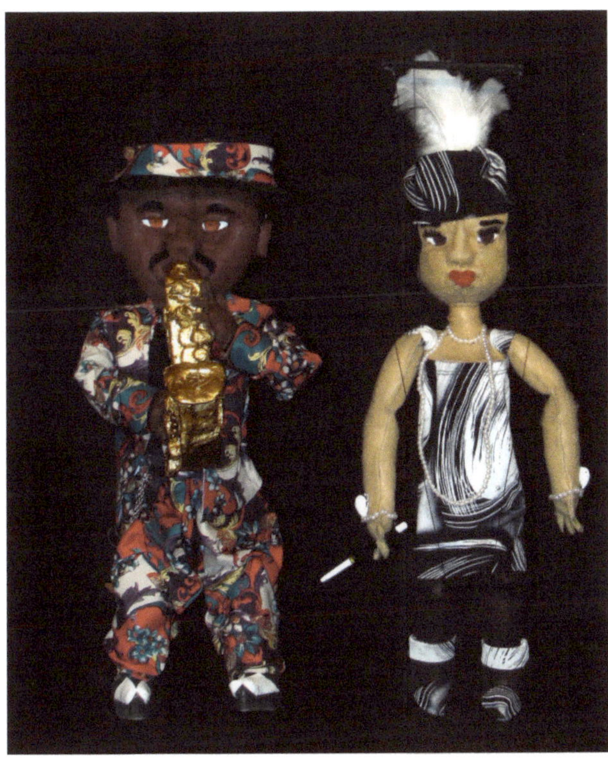

Reinvention of Chess, mixed media puppet chess pieces, by students participating in Chameleon Arts and Youth Development programming, 2008.

and that they need to be capturing the discussion and producing multiple ideas.

One group is selected, and each member is asked what they contributed to the discussion. Frequently, one or two from each group will say, "Nothing." They are then asked why this happened, and the class is asked to consider how the process could have been more inclusive. How could they have invented a way to make every one give their opinion on the problem.

Then I give everyone these directions to follow prior to brainstorming for the second round:

- Each person is to write down five ideas regarding the assignment prior to discussion. When the discussion begins, they are required to follow a statement with a question. For example, the exercise could start with this question: "I think chess should be played by live people in a field. What do you think?" Everyone else has to respond before the beginning person can participate in the conversation. The statement and question rule prioritizes listener action and sets up a dialogue that demands multiple responses rather than single, pre-determined, conclusions. The groups return to collaborative brainstorming following these directions and concerns.
- Each person in their group is required to take accurate notes or visuals on the dialogue and make a list of opportunities. Four pairs of listening ears are better than one, so we do not assign a single person to be the secretary.
- Convincing others to articulate their ideas is a priority over the communication of your own ideas in detail.
- Each group is to present 20 ideas, five from each participant.

Step Two:
Now is the time to categorize and evaluate potential content.

Each group is to discuss the 20 ideas and narrow the list to five. The groups are told to evaluate whether ideas can be combined, or if one can evolve into and support another one. What are the most interesting ideas? Are some of them overviews and others details? Do some of them fit together, while others do not seem as useful at this time?

Then the groups are asked to organize a presentation of their process. Describe how they developed multiple ideas, how they evaluated them and how the field of ideas was eventually reduced from 20 to five.

Step Three:

The remaining 20 ideas are written on the chalk or dry erase board and each group is asked to give their presentation of their ideas and the process of coming up with the ideas. The whole class votes on the best three ideas and suggests changes to further refine them. At this stage the assignment is completed.

Step Four:

We then ask these questions as a follow up:

- Can discarded ideas from the exercises solve other problems?
- What can we find out from reconsidering the discarded ideas?

This focus of this discussion is to reinforce the consideration of multiple ideas and the process of brainstorming.

This is the end of the assignment. A final conclusion is not reached with this exercise.

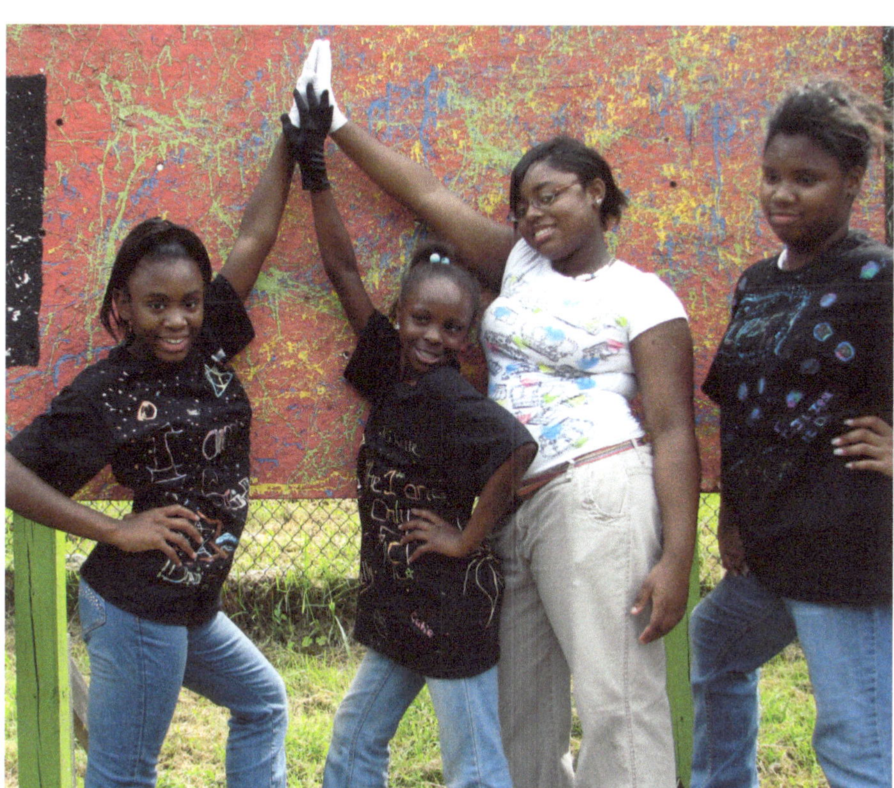

Chameleon dance group, *Happy Feet*, Kansas City, Missouri, 2005.

Chapter 11
Activities and Projects

Public Spaces and Private Studio Practice: How do the Two Intersect?

Turning individual studio investigation into a process that both balances expression and opens the door to social practice is the outcome of a series of assignments that are based in teamwork, performance and installation.

We have worked to balance the needs for the student to work independently and as a team in both the Printmaking and the Foundation Departments at the Kansas City Art Institute. The faculty has designed a number of projects that begin as an individual studio investigation and end with a collaborative installation or performance, rather than a gallery exhibition of individual work.

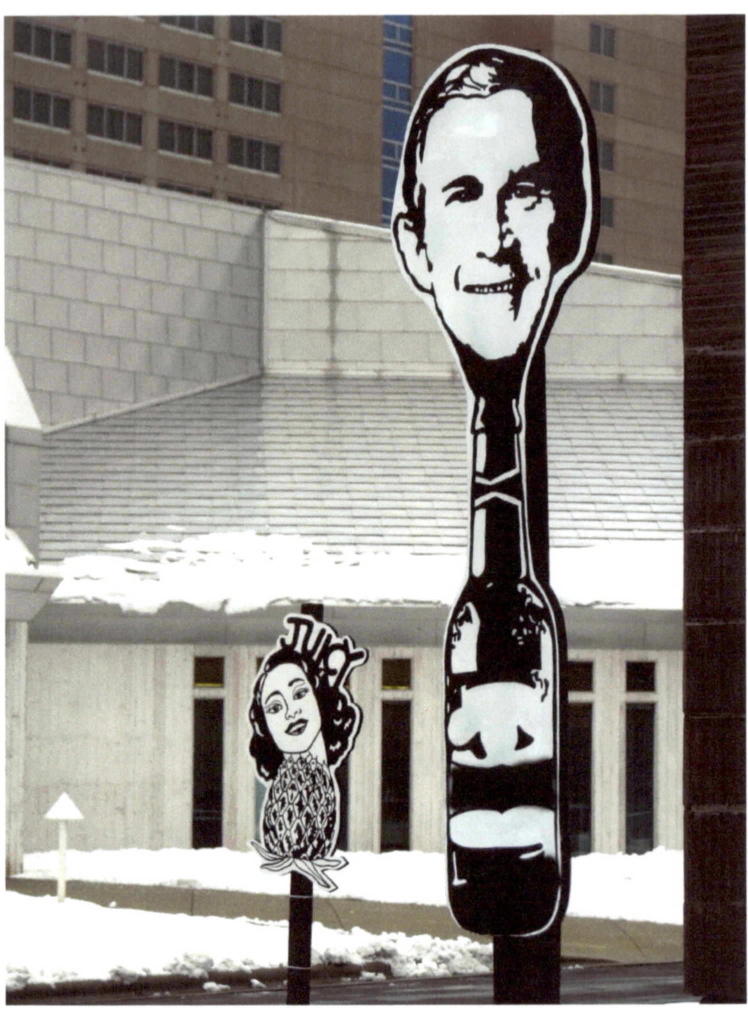

Consumer Heads, student collaborative project which is part of the Foundation Department studies at the Kansas City Art Institute, Kansas City, Missouri, 2009.

Consumer Heads

This project begins with a 2' x 4' sheet of multiple density fiberboard (MDF) that is 3/4" thick. Students are asked to design a shaped piece based on a collage, combining a single human head and typical consumer products such as: toasters, mixers, guns, cars and related household items. The final collage is to be made into a black-and-white graphic, scaled up on the board with the outside shape cutout of the design. Each graphic shaped MDF image is to be connected to an 8' tall, 2' x 4' stake, so it can be installed as a free-standing sign.

The works are installed in public spaces as a group display. Resources for the collages are advertisements from the early 20th century through the 1960s. The student is asked to first, collect the image resources and then create 10 collages, using either Photoshop or traditional cutting and pasting.

Even though each sign is made by a different student the visual qualities in the pieces are similar to each other, so they look as if they were all created by a single artist. This pulls the work together visually, so it functions well as a coherent statement. The signs are then taken around the city and displayed at various street festivals, as well as on the campus of KCAI. This helps them to reach a broad public audience.

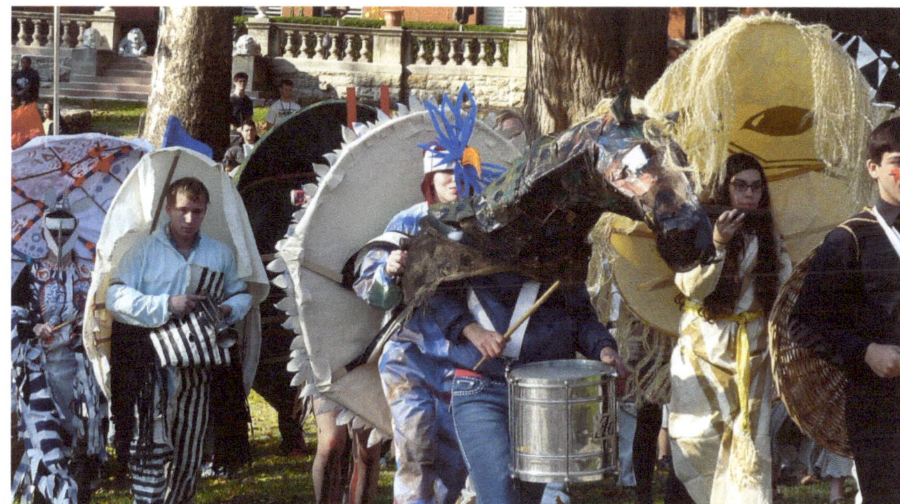

Day of the Dead Trees, parade facilitated by Professor Russell Ferguson at the Kansas City Art Institute, November, 2011.

Parade: Day of the Dead Trees

Russell Ferguson, Chair of the Foundation Department at the Kansas City Art Institute, has developed a remarkable project that invites all of the freshman foundation students to participate in a public event. Brazilian carnival is the inspiration for this project. Ferguson ties together several ideas to create the theme for *Day of the Dead Trees.*

Closely associated with the *Day of the Dead* festival in Mexico, the festivities are combined with the celebration of the fall harvest in North America, accompanied by traditional carnival drumming. The students are asked to use cardboard, paper, cloth, hot glue and simple modes of construction to create sculptural costumes for a parade. Standard pop culture content cannot be included. The students study the amazing costumes of Burkina Faso African tribes, as well as other cultural resources in preparation for construction of the pieces.

One of the region's top drummers and artistic director of the Traditional Music Society, Bird Flemming, teaches the students call and response drumming and chanting, based on Brazilian samba music. The students practice marching and drumming for several weeks until the project concludes with a walk across the campus of KCAI to the Nelson-Atkins Museum of Art. The students enter the museum, walk through the main hall, and out the front door. Hundreds of people line the parade route for the annual event. Once again, fundamentals of collaborative creativity are stressed, demonstrating that the dynamics of a group of committed artists can produce magical events far beyond the capability of a single person.

Traditional art audiences have been associated with exclusionary aesthetics based on criticism and evaluation of style and content. *The Day of the Dead Trees* and *Consumer Heads* take the artistic action to a broad general audience who experience the work as a new and meaningful ritual. *The Day of the Dead Trees* helps to move art and students into a paradigm where the artist becomes the designer of new mythologies by considering these principles:

- In teaching collaboration, skills and experiences are woven together in a series of classroom assignments that combine lecture, creative activities and discussion.
- The focus is often not on the quality of the final work but on the process. The exercises are not graded or critiqued in the traditional manner.
- In an activity with a non-arts community, the work is not critiqued but supported, encouraged and celebrated.
- Reflecting on the work and the creative process involved in producing art is important

for artists and non-artists.

These first exercises are approached in the same manner, evaluating individuals using these collaborative criteria:

- Listening
- Supporting others
- Helping others articulate their thoughts and ideas

Survey, Question and Response

A simple method for collecting information for an arts project is to create a survey. The answers to the questions become the data from which the art can be produced. Businesses, political groups, scientists and others use polls to retrieve information about specific groups of people. They use the information to hone a message, design products or analyze how a group thinks or lives. In social arts practice, the survey can either be a serious attempt to understand qualities of a specific group or it can be random, entertaining or whimsical. The students use the survey as a means of engagement for people in a public space such as a bar, coffee shop or art gallery. The survey itself has two distinct roles:

- An artistic process which gathers content.
- A product intended to be the exhibited outcome.

Two of the first techniques needed to engage people are collecting information and then stimulating participation between strangers using the same public or commercial space.

Encourage a discussion of strategies for collecting information and stimulating engagement. Ask the students to create a one-page survey, 8.5" x 11", and have the local copy shop print them as tear-off pads, similar to post-it notes.

Divide the class into groups of four people each, and make each group responsible for creating their own survey. The groups are to find an establishment and gain permission to place the survey pads where customers can easily fill them out. The groups each design collections boxes or pin-up boards where people can drop off their surveys.

In the past, students have worked with tattoo parlors, bike shops, skateboard shops, bars, coffee shops and community centers.

After two weeks of monitoring and documenting people at the selected location, the surveys are collected. The next step is to use the data to produce a response, which they post at the place of business for others to see.

The students can utilize the surveys to create books with prelude text to outline the project so the people that go to the coffeeshop or bar can read, laugh and discuss their responses.

When the surveys ask for visual responses as well as written responses, individual pages can be blown up and printed as large digital prints. These are then installed as posters. Sometimes the survey responses are collated and the information is turned into a large edition of silkscreen prints. These are posted on telephone poles and in other public spaces. Black-line prints from a local blueprint store, 3' x 6', were put up in the windows of a coffeeshop. Under other circumstances, the information was used for a gallery installation, and the patrons of the establishment were invited to attend.

The majority of the time the surveys created included questions that are slightly embarrassing and meant to encourage storytelling. The questions are evaluated on the hope that they will help people to share by encouraging conversation.

Coffeeshop Survey Ideas:

- In three sentences, tell about a time your mother embarrassed you.

- How old were you when you lost your virginity?

- What have you stolen from a friend?

- On a scale of 1-10, are you a kind person?

- Do you go to the bathroom in front of your lover?

- What do you think about while waiting for a stoplight to turn green? Sex, yourself, your job, nature, God, vampires, road kill, love?

Question and Response

Harrell Fletcher is on the faculty of the Portland State University Department of Art and was a participant in the 2004 Whitney Biennial at the Whitney Museum of American Art in New York, NY. In collaboration with Miranda July and Yuri Ono, Fletcher founded the website *Learning to Love You More* in 2002. The focus of the project was to come up with new ideas to stimulate artistic and creative action as a part of daily life. Each day, a new assignment was posted on the website, and visitors were invited to participate by following the instructions and sending in the requested work, which was then posted. Knowledge of the website spread as people sent the link to others, and in time over 5,000 people around the world had finished assignments. The responses to the questions were stunning in their insight and creativity. There is hilarity in many of the responses. Here are some examples of their assignments:

Assignment 50: Take a flash photo under your bed.
Assignment 54: Draw the news.
Assignment 55: Photograph a significant outfit.
Assignment 39: Take a picture of your parents kissing.[1]

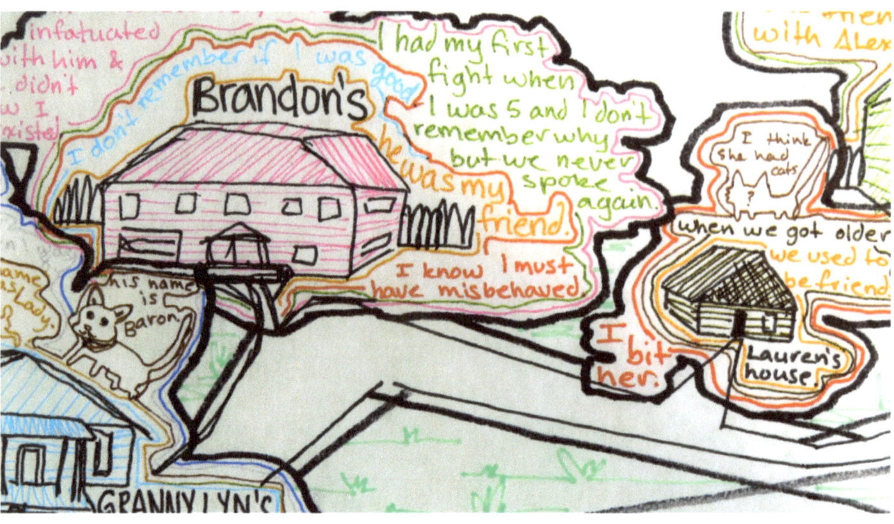

Laura Frazier, *First Neighborhood*, Kansas City Art Institute class project, 2014.

Visualization

Working with research collected from an organization or information source such as the report on youth homelessness in Kansas City, Kansas, presents a major problem for an artist or designer. How do we effectively communicate and process visually complex and quantitative information?

In the various projects proposed by Harrell Fletcher, Dr. Eric Avery or the Guerilla Girls, the intent is to provide the public with data that supports either a political point of view or makes others aware of important resources that are available to them. The student or artist must begin to deal with fundamental strategies for analytical design.

These activities are strongly related to Edward Tufte's *The Visual Display of Quantitative Information*,[2] so it is important that the student has a fundamental knowledge of processes related to evaluation of evidence and visual data, such as graphs, tables and sparklines.

Artists often find themselves working with complex relationships. An understanding of the language of data graphics provides tools for the communication of these complex ideas. This exercise provides an experiential basis for mapping information.

First Neighborhood

To introduce students to data graphics on an experiential and personal level, we use Chameleon Arts and Youth Development's *Portrait of Self* journaling curriculum designed to help collect quantitative information and re-kindle lost memories as a resource for arts actions. The first prompt given to the class is: "Draw a map of your first or primary neighborhood and mark on it all the places you were bad." The participating group is asked to create a drawing showing the houses, buildings, streets,and open areas that comprise their neighborhood. They are then asked to map their past actions and to articulate what constitutes bad behavior. After the initial response to the first question, they expand their mapping activities and mark positions on the map where they did other things. A series of other data questions are then added:

- Which houses had dogs, cats, birds, or other animals?

- Where did the older people live, and where were the weird people?
- Who bought a new car?
- Did you have a special secret place to play?
- Where was the closest drug house, church or liquor store?
- What were the names of your friends?
- Who was the first friend you got into a fight with?
- Who did you have a crush on?
- Where was your first kiss?

When the maps are completed, the students tell in-depth stories about themselves, bringing the class together and creating an environment of care and trust. The maps are then quantified by turning them into charts and graphs. Working together, we ask the students to record as much information from the maps as possible. They can then create charts that show the student's economic class, race, background and religion. The students are instructed to make a chart that shows how many people in the class lived in the inner city, suburbs or rural areas. The charts show how many people lived in their primary neighborhood all of their lives, who moved, and how often. The maps also reflected how many families rented or owned their own homes. "Was your neighborhood integrated, a mono-culture, diverse, or restricted?"

The students' documentation of their neighborhoods emphasizes the makeup of their collective past and fosters a discussion about their personal concerns. The graphics calculate information and provide an overview of the social and economic makeup of the class. This exercise allows them to see themselves both as a demographic and as a group of contemporaries.

Telling the Stories of Other: Interviews

The importance of storytelling in creating social change cannot be underestimated. It is through stories that the facts regarding homelessness, hunger, pain and joy become personal. A statistic is valuable as a point for measuring a problem or condition, but illustrating that point through a personal story makes it empathetic, helping others to understand it. Through the power of helping others tell their stories, we can help to build a better world with healthier communities.

We have facilitated a number of projects by helping others to tell their stories, including homeless children, Jewish and African-American geriatric patients and survivors of the Holocaust. We start with a discussion on how to interview the folks we will be working with. Large historical questions do not help recall a hidden or deep personal memory, but smaller specific questions lead to stories that help the person being interviewed share the truth of their reality. Here are some examples:

- How did your experience in the Vietnam War change your life?
- How did you deal with Jim Crow laws?
- Do you remember a friend's family whose son or daughter went to Vietnam?
- Do you remember when a white man or woman called you "boy?"
- Where did you buy toys? Was there a toy you wanted that you could not have?
- Did your mom give you money to go to the store? Did you ever lose it?
- Was there a dog in the neighborhood that frightened you?
- Do you remember your father or mother embarrassing you?

Each of these questions presents an opportunity to segue to larger social and political issues. The subject of a toy someone wanted but could not have opens issues of parenting, class and value.

Working with Holocaust survivors at Village Shalom in Overland Park, Kansas, we asked a man if he remembered a green grocer in his small Polish village. You could see him light up as he began to remember his village and describe where the store was located. He also talked about the Kosher butcher and other various stores along the main road of his village. He paused for a long moment and told the story of the last time he saw his little sister, the day when the men and boys were taken away from the village by Nazi soldiers. He softly said her name and told us that he had not said her name aloud in over 60 years.

Interview Timeline

We have learned from experience that having students interview diverse populations without research or a timeline of events does not engender trust or stories. We determined that when working with geriatric residents an 80-year time line of cultural and historical events was needed, as well as a general understanding of the history of the particular group.

There is important cultural information hidden in interviews and surveys that can easily be missed. In 2002, while working with the Swope Geriatrics Center, it was not expected that the subject of baseball would be of particular importance to the residents. Without exception, they had all mentioned Jackie Robinson breaking the color barrier as one of the most exciting public events in their lives. This important detail escaped us until our post interview discussions.

On our second project with Swope Village Geriatrics Center, a mostly African-American facility, the time line started in 1931. We then looked for significant events that would have been important for that time period to an African-American population. Through experience we had learned that a person in the center if born in 1931 would be 80 years old. They would have been 27 when Jackie Robinson broke the color barrier in Major League Baseball, playing for the Brooklyn Dodgers. When we asked the folks about Robinson, they got excited and remembered it well. All of the residents told stories expressing both fear and pride in relation to this event. The question built trust between a group of white kids and teachers and the African-American residents.

Village Shalom: Collaboration with Residents

The Kansas City Jewish Museum of Contemporary Art (KCJMCA) provides exhibitions and related programming with the goal of engaging senior and diverse audiences. It is housed in Village Shalom retirement home in Overland Park, Kansas.[3] Here is one art student's experience working with an elderly resident on art therapy fundraising projects:

Grilled green beans and freshly baked bread was the aroma. And butter. The large doors swung open with the whoosh of a controlled climate building, where all the air is filtered before it goes outside. The food smelled better than most restaurants I was able to frequent at the time, and the 10:30 a.m. arrival time always made my caffeine invested stomach positively hurt. After I left the class, I stopped for bagels and more coffee at the Einstein Brother's bagel shop just down the street.

Our room was up the elevator and down the hall from the Epsten Gallery. We sometimes stopped there in the morning, before everyone had arrived for class to look at the exhibits. We found our classroom, turned the lock, and opened a white cabinet made to mimic a kitchen. Here we found watercolor paints, markers, charcoal sticks and pencils. The paper was in the next partition next to the sink.

Some of the people we worked with were holocaust survivors. Their tattoos were faded and marred, but still starkly visible in the winter light of morning in Overland Park, Kansas. They were dark, teal-blue in color, although some had a mottled green or black element to them.

She sat directly across from me on the second day. The assistant wheeled her in to the first available spot, let out a short breath, turned and walked away quickly. Rhoda glared at me immediately. "Aren't you too old for school, honey?" she challenged me. I was just hungry enough to quip back "You're older than me." The bread and butter smell was back.

It was the beginning of a friendship that lasted for over two years. We drew flowers, baskets, art from the gallery, and other people in the art therapy class together. We talked about being too old to live and being too old for school. She told me I was good at drawing, but she thought I could lose my husband over this, which I needed to think about. I should be at home, since I had a kid.

Social practice art, like all art, is besieged by speculation and the theories of academics. This analysis can shed light for students theorizing on different strands of thought or working on a paper or presentation. As a facilitator working with elderly participants, I wasn't able to remember any theory or even the group of questions I had planned on asking. Picking out watercolors and paper, setting up a still life, and picking out markers and pencils all took on the feel of a familiar ritual, a mundane beginning to a transformative couple of months. As Sandra Hayes and Lyle Yorks state in their book Arts and Societal Learning: Transforming Communities Socially, Politically and Culturally, participation in the arts serves to pull people into a "learning space" where people can empower themselves, as opposed to finding influence in an outside environment.[3] Art also has the ability to confront conflict in a positive manner, which helped me on my journey into geriatric interactions.

Cantankerous and confrontational, Rhoda was very transparent about her frustrations, which were numerous. Working together, we were able to channel these mindsets and situations into visually literate drawings and paintings. Sadness and frustration were clearly visible in some of the pieces.

The experience of working with Rhoda taught me that what I learned as a facilitator was as important as what she learned as an arts student. Through the arts, a situation was created where two people who had nearly conflicting personalities were able to work creatively and constructively. We actually learned to like each other, which was a result I didn't expect. Later, images we created together were made into greeting cards that were sold in the gift shop.

One day we spent 20 minutes of the session looking for flowers to paint that were up to Rhoda's standards. She disliked the ones that had started to wilt.

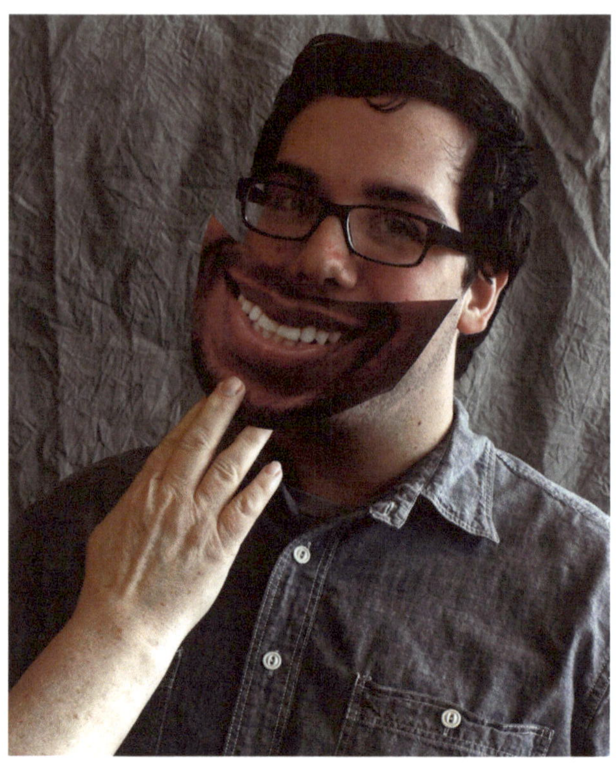

Hugh Merrill, *Mix Up* at *ArtWorkers: Creativity and America*, at the George A. Spiva Art Center, Joplin, Missouri, 2013.

Chameleon Arts and Youth Development worked with *America: Now and Here* in the summer of 2011 at the Leedy-Voulkos Art Center in Kansas City, Missouri. The following projects were designed for and performed at the event. Variations of this project eventually led to the *Artworkers: Creativity and America,* exhibition at the George A. Spiva Center for the Arts in Joplin, Mo.

MIX Up: The American Family

A series of photographs of people with differing racial, ethnic, and cultural backgrounds is the first step of this investigation. At the Leedy-Voulkos event, various genders and ages, from babies to seniors, were all represented. Digitally printed photos, just a little larger than their true proportions, were cut into three strips: eyes, nose and mouth areas. The photos were traced onto cardboard, which was then cut out into corresponding face shapes. The photos were glued to a cardboard backing, making a sturdy "mask."

A photographic studio with a backdrop and lights was set up in the gallery as a workshop location. Participating photographers invited the visitors to hold up the "diversity masks" to their own face to fashion a new American-hybrid face. The photographs were then uploaded onto our Facebook and Flickr pages, where the participants could download them. The photos could be enlarged to become a gallery exhibition at a participating community center or museum. Visitors were encouraged to participate in the event by bringing their own cameras to shoot photographs of their friends and families when our professional photographers were not available.

MAKE A BETTER PRESIDENT

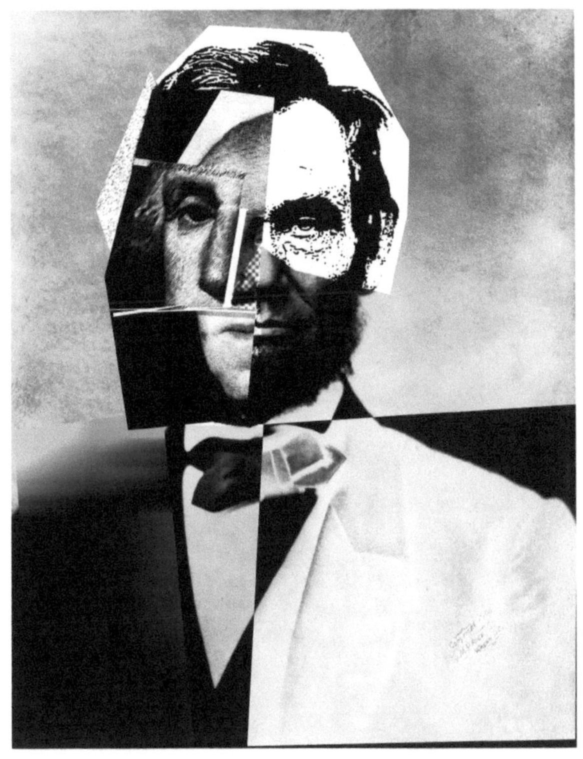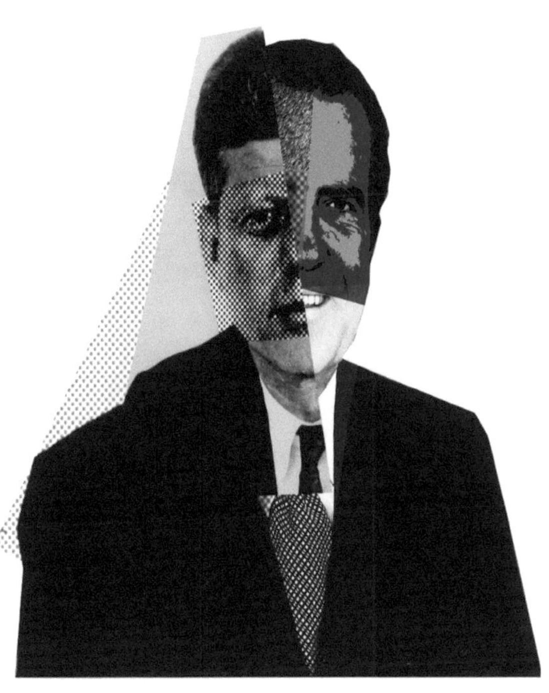

Hugh Merrill, *Make a Better President* at *Art Workers: Creativity and America,* at the George A. Spiva Art Center, Joplin, Missouri, 2013.

Creating a Better President

The public was invited to create their own "better presidents" by building collages made from the faces of our presidents, presidential candidates, celebrities and other public figures. To facilitate the project, we provided the participants with Xerox copies of presidential portraits. Pre-printed images of these celebrities and heads of state were included: John Kennedy, Richard Nixon, Maya Angelou, Jimmy Carter, James Brown, Ronald Reagan, Bill Clinton, George Bush and Barack Obama.

The public was invited to a Saturday workshop where artists/facilitators worked with kids and the general public. The pre-printed copies of the faces were cut up and reconstructed into images of their perfect leader. There was a copier in the gallery space so the participants could enlarge or reduce the images if they wanted to. When the participants completed their "better president" collages, they were asked copy their work and pin it to the exhibition wall set aside for the project. By the end of the four-hour workshop, there were over 100 new presidents; all were a combination of both the right and left of Democratic and Republican personalities. The project could be extended to an online process asking people to use portraits of the presidents to create a collage image of their leader of choice. They were then invited to upload their portrayal to a Facebook page or website for exhibition.

We started the project by taking a postcard-style photograph of the Statue of Liberty. We enhanced the image in Photoshop and then had it printed as a large 5' x 10' vinyl banner.

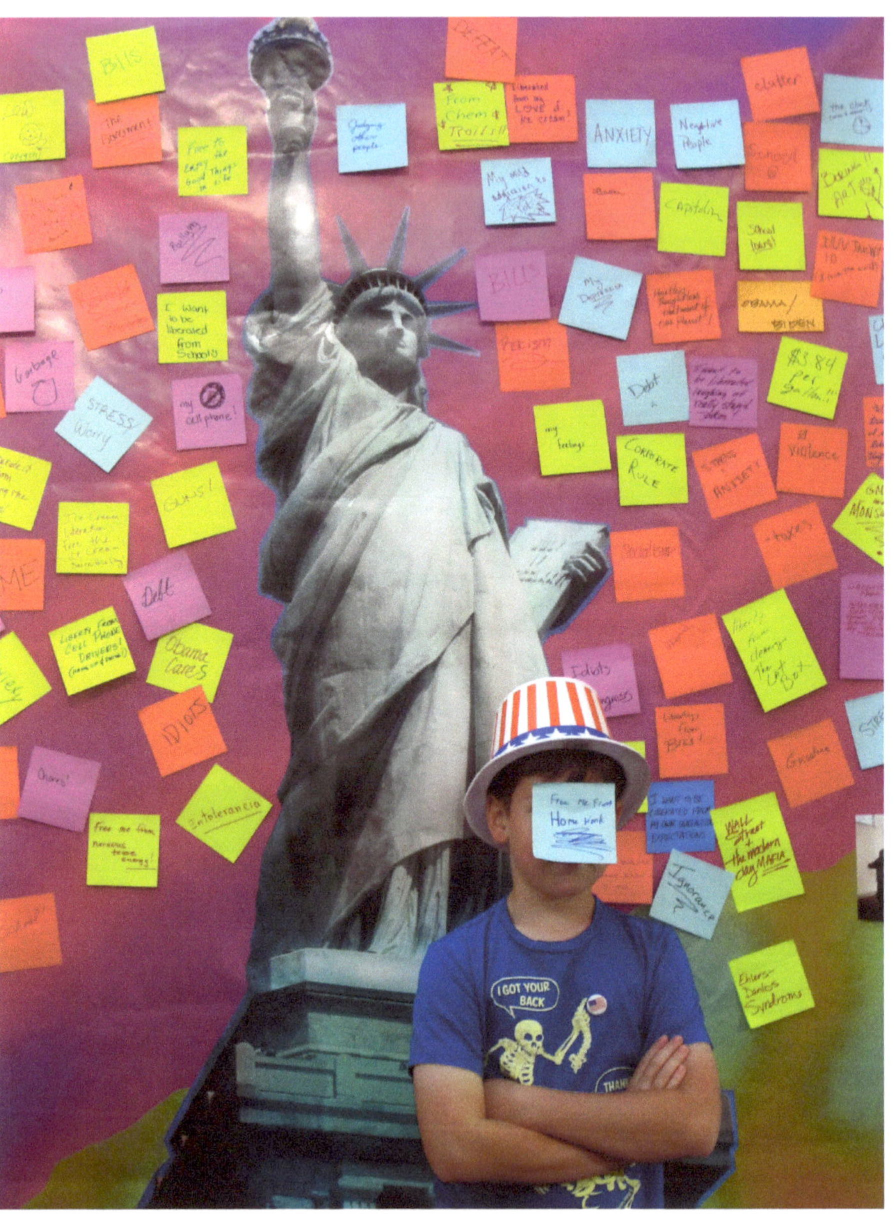

Statues of Liberty

A photography studio was set up in the gallery with the banners as backdrops for the workshop. Participating photographers invited the visitors to select objects from a table laden with Americana: small flags, Uncle Sam hats, American eagles and similar items. There were also pens and markers so people could write on large sticky notes the answer to this question: "What do you want to be freed from?"

The sticky notes were applied to the vinyl banner so everyone could read them. Folks then stood in front of the banners and had their photographs taken. These portraits were uploaded onto our Facebook and Flickr pages where the participants could download them. The banner has appeared at street festivals, regional museums, and at fundraising events for the Coalition Against Human Trafficking.

Great American Zine

Participants were provided with pre-printed zine pages with images of American icons such as Lincoln engravings, flags, eagles, cannons, cornucopias and other images of traditional Americana. On each pre-printed page were these questions:

- Name one thing to make "your" America better.
- What is your American Dream?
- Fill in new words to America the Beautiful: "Oh beautiful for spacious ____________, for _______ waves of __________, for purple mountain __________________."

The participants were encouraged to cut up the pages and recombine the images and questions into new pages to create their own version. Art supplies were provided. CAYD artists worked at the tables, and their presence encouraged the audience to join the experience.

A copier was provided so that the participants could copy their pages and leave them as part of the exhibition, as well as take a copy with them. The process of collage with short assignments and questions, coupled with the ability to participate with others, helped to engage the mostly non-arts audience.

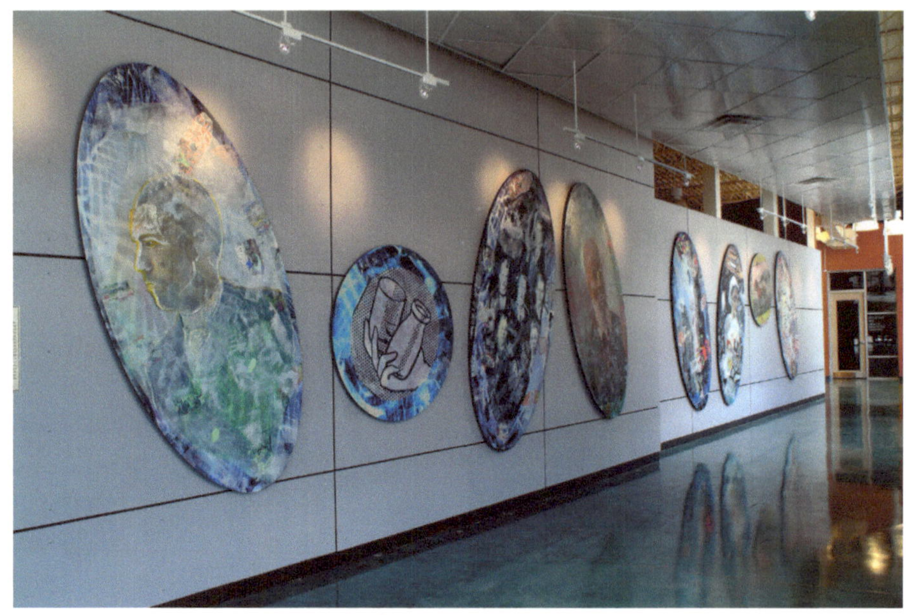

Art of Memory, at the Sanford-Kimpton Health Facility, Columbia, Missouri, 1% for the arts commission, 2002-2004.

Projects 1996-2012

The following projects demonstrate the processes and utilization of assignments discussed in this book.

Art of Memory (2002-2004)

In 2002, Hugh Merrill was commissioned to produce artwork for the Sanford-Kimpton Health Facility in Columbia, Missouri, which was completed in 2004. Designated as a percent-for-art public project, Merrill and Chameleon Arts and Youth Development (CAYD) artists used their *Portrait of Self* journaling curriculum and process to collect personal stories and family information from the doctors, staff and folks that used this center. From the mass of personal information, the artists created large graphic collages that were digitally printed and installed throughout the various clinics and spaces in the building. The images resonate as artwork for the broader public and represent cherished memorabilia for the personnel working in the building.

Dania Beach Elementary School (1999-2000)

Working in conjunction with the Hollywood, Florida, Center for the Arts, CAYD and Hugh Merrill were invited to create a mural on the front of the Dania Beach Elementary School. The project began by collecting visual information and family memorabilia from students and their families. Photographic portraits of the students were used to create a collaborative graphic mural installed across the outside of the school buildings, creating the illusion that the children are looking out at their neighborhood. The mural had a positive effect on the neighborhood, bringing people out and stopping the prostitution and drug activity previously common in the area.

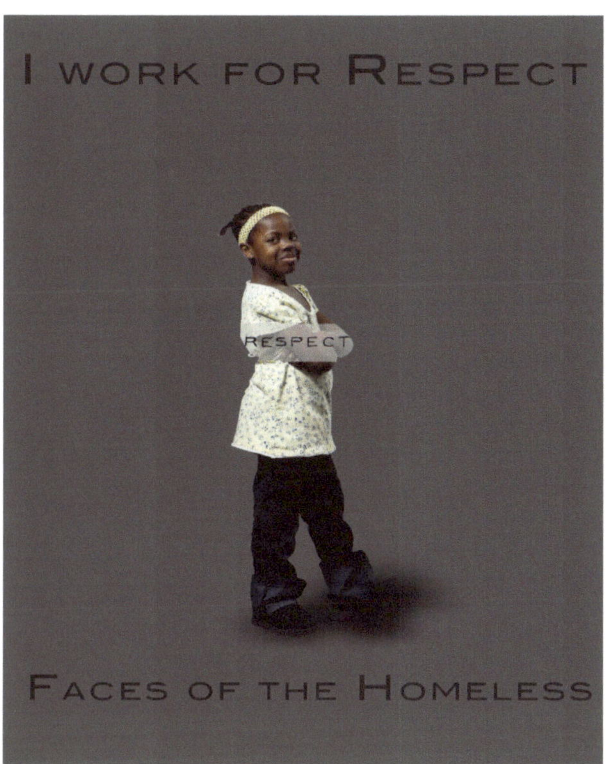

Faces of the Homeless, a project in conjunction with the Liaison for Homeless Children, Kansas City, Kansas, 2009.

Faces of the Homeless (2008)

When we think of the Homeless, we often envision a tattered older man holding a sign by the off ramp of a highway. The reality is far different. The average age of a homeless person in Kansas City, Kansas is seven years old. In order to bring this story to a broader public audience, CAYD undertook the arts project, *Faces of Homeless Youth.* The goal of this project was to increase the self-image of homeless teens in Kansas City, while enhancing public understanding of the impact of homelessness on children and youth.

Working in collaboration, the Kansas City, Kansas Public Schools Homeless Liaison, Staci Pratt and Chameleon artists guided a group of homeless teenagers living and going to school in Wyandotte County. The students created journals, art and performance projects from 2007 to 2010. This work led to the production of a series of posters and large-scale graphic images of the youth installed at the Willa Gill Resource Center, in Kansas City, Kansas, since June 20, 2008. The posters help people connect with the reality of homelessness. The arts programming provided the children with skills to develop a coherent and insightful artistic voice. The programming also served to support their academic learning, self-esteem, and active involvement.

Seldom do homeless communities have the opportunity to participate in the arts or have positive images of themselves exhibited in soup kitchens and resource centers where they go for help and food. The homeless people using the Willa Gill resource center is excited and proud to cherish the artwork featuring images of their children. Work and images were produced by artists Hugh Merrill, Matt Hilger and Patrick Moonasar.

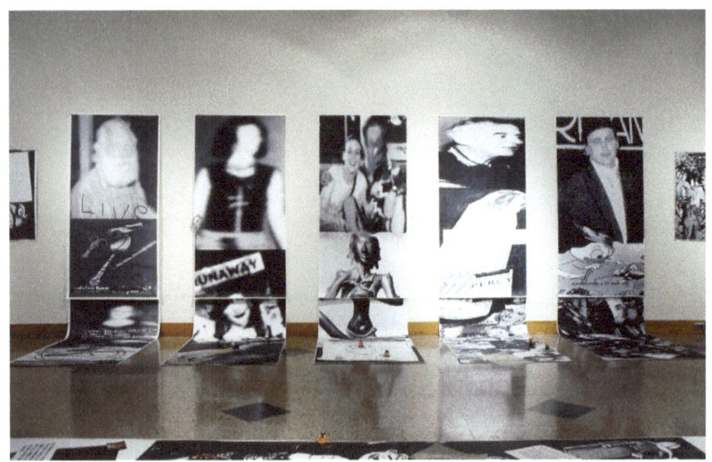

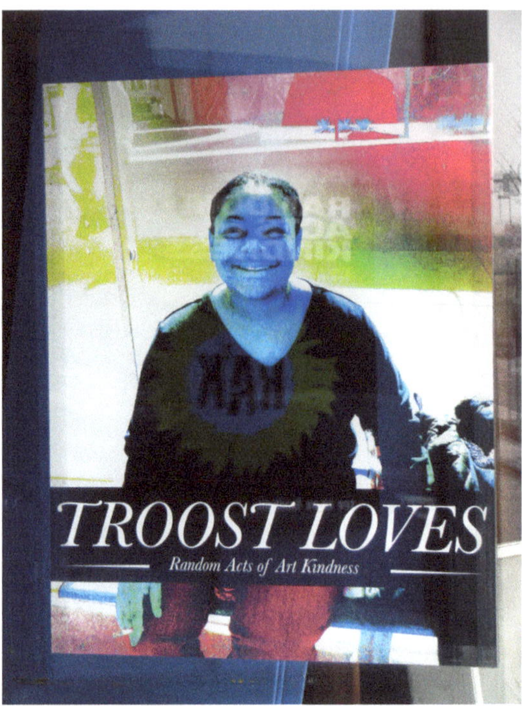

Daum Museum (2001)

The Daum Museum is located on the campus of State Fair Community College in Sedalia, Missouri. Hugh Merrill and Chameleon Arts were invited to produce a series of large-scale narrative black-line prints that captured the memorabilia of everyday folks in the region.

Family photographs, notes from high school students, doodles, and other ephemera were copied and then reprinted as large collages. These pieces were scanned into a large-scale black line copier, where they were copied and then placed on the walls where they eventually spilled over onto the floor of the gallery. Tables with art supplies were set up so the public could participate by adding their stories to the exhibit.

Random Acts of Kindness (2011)

In 2011, a group of art students at the Kansas City Art Institute designed a project to add joy to the routines of people catching the bus at 31st Street and Troost Avenue in Kansas City, Missouri.

Troost is the historical dividing line that during the Jim Crow era of American apartheid separated African-Americans from the neighboring working-class whites. The folks riding the bus were served coffee on cold February mornings and given apples to snack on. The students also set up a book exchange and provided commuter art bags filled with games, drawings and poetry.

They took photographic portraits of the commuters and turned the photos into large-scale graphic posters that were displayed in the storefronts behind and near the bus stops, turning the street into a gallery. The riders were the subjects in the displayed posters. The project has continued in a variety of forms as a street gallery for over three years.

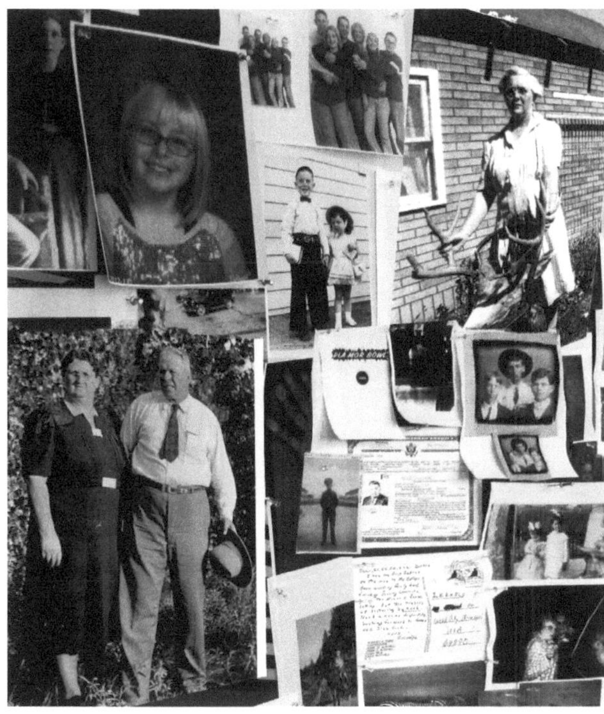

Hugh Merrill, *Stories: Place and Families* at *Art-Workers: Creativity and America*, at the George A. Spiva Art Center, Joplin, Missouri, 2013.

Studio 150 and Kauffman Foundation (2002)

Kansas City area high school students were selected to participate in a summer program inspired by the highly successful Studio 39 program in Chicago. CAYD artists Josie Mai and Hugh Merrill used the Portrait of Self journaling process to create content for a series of street graphics. Students were asked to make visuals representing their hopes and dreams for the future. They created collages out of their report cards, class notes, tests and other personal ephemera. The resulting pieces were printed on the same material used for floor advertising graphics in warehouses or big-box stores, a thick durable material. The collages were installed on the sidewalks in front of the Kauffman Foundation Conference Center in Kansas City, Missouri. Most of the participants were high school kids from inner city public schools; most of them were African-American or Latino, two demographics that are often quickly stereotyped. The installation of prints on the walkways outside the Kauffman Center created a safe zone for visitors to learn about teenagers that have been perceived as frightening because of common societal stereotypes.

Our City: Ourselves (1998)

In 1998, Merrill collaborated with conceptual artist Christian Boltanski in conjunction with his exhibition at the Kemper Museum of Contemporary Art in Kansas City, Missouri. The socially relevant aspect of the exhibition was a city-wide project conceived at a meeting in New York City. Boltanski's goal was to create a newspaper circular that invited the metropolitan area residents to the museum. The idea was for the audience to take over the gallery so that their input would become the exhibition itself.

At the time, Boltanski was interested in objects that had become orphans due to the loss of their owners: clothes, objects, cleaning supplies, a series of everyday objects.

Merrill's background as a print artist led him to suggest that copier machines be placed in the gallery to encourage the public to copy something belonging to them and place it on the gallery walls. Boltanski continued the idea to include having folks copy their family memorabilia. The entire population of Kansas City was invited to bring their family photographs and memorabilia, which would be copied and exhibited on the gallery walls. Designer Bruce MacIntosh and Hugh Merrill designed a newspaper circular (similar to a retail ad) that was distributed in the Sunday edition of the Kansas City Star newspaper, inviting the public to participate. This suggestion was similar

to Boltanski's process of working with photographs, clothes and other objects left behind by people, some of whom had died.

In a similar manner to the *Artworkers: Creativity and America* exhibition, thousands of people brought in documents and photographs. The pieces were Xeroxed and pinned salon style to the pristine walls of the museum. Six large comment books were set up on pedestals in the gallery so people could respond to the work.

On the walls were the Xerox copies of Yiddish diary pages from Poland dated from 1938, graduation pictures of high school students from the 1940s, and World War II ration cards. Many residents brought in their photographs, some of which dated back to the Civil War. People reconnected with each other through the installation and recorded their finds in the comment books. Boltanski noted that the people spent more time looking at the rows of photocopies than they did gazing on his work in the other gallery space. He had achieved his goal of turning the museum over to the city's residents, by-passing the curatorial and aesthetic standards common in institutions. Boltanski's work is often about the disappearance of identity. He told Merrill: "You die twice in life, once when you drop dead and once when no one can recognize a photo of you."

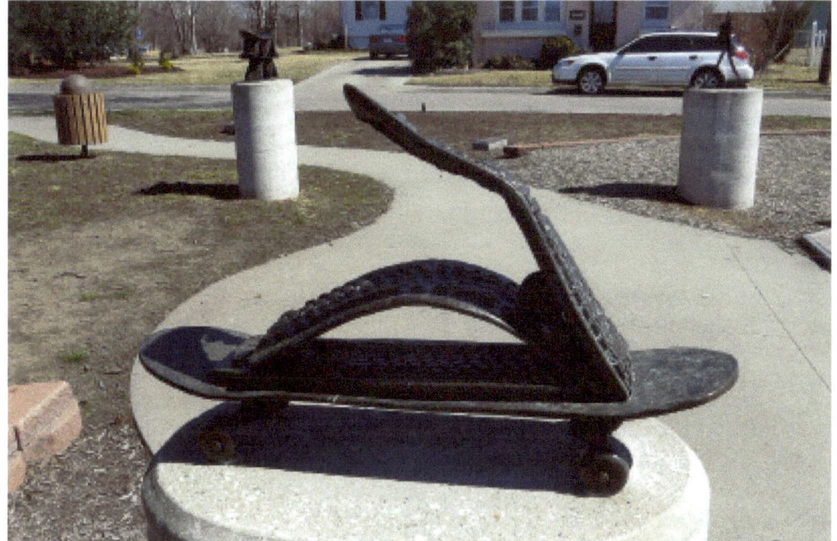

Hugh Merrill and Adelia Ganson, *Skate: Roeland Park*, installation view of bronze sculptures, in Roeland Park, Kansas, 2004.

Skate: Roeland Park (2004)

Since 1948, Chameleon Arts and Youth Development has worked with kids. Kids loved to be amused, and skateboarding is an activity that crosses nearly all ages and demographic groups. On a nice day in everywhere, USA, you can see groups of kids toting skateboards with them, with some jumping on and some jumping off of them. Through this common actitvity, Chameleon artists designed bronze sculptures on pedestals for a skate park in Roeland Park, Kansas. The sculptures are paired with quotes and interactive verses encouraging people think about poetry and their surroundings. While some of the verses focus on action and consideration, others encourage reflection and self-awareness. The park project was created and sponsored by a local businessman as well as a non-profit arts organization to both beautify the space, and encourage a creative thought process.

Portrait of Self

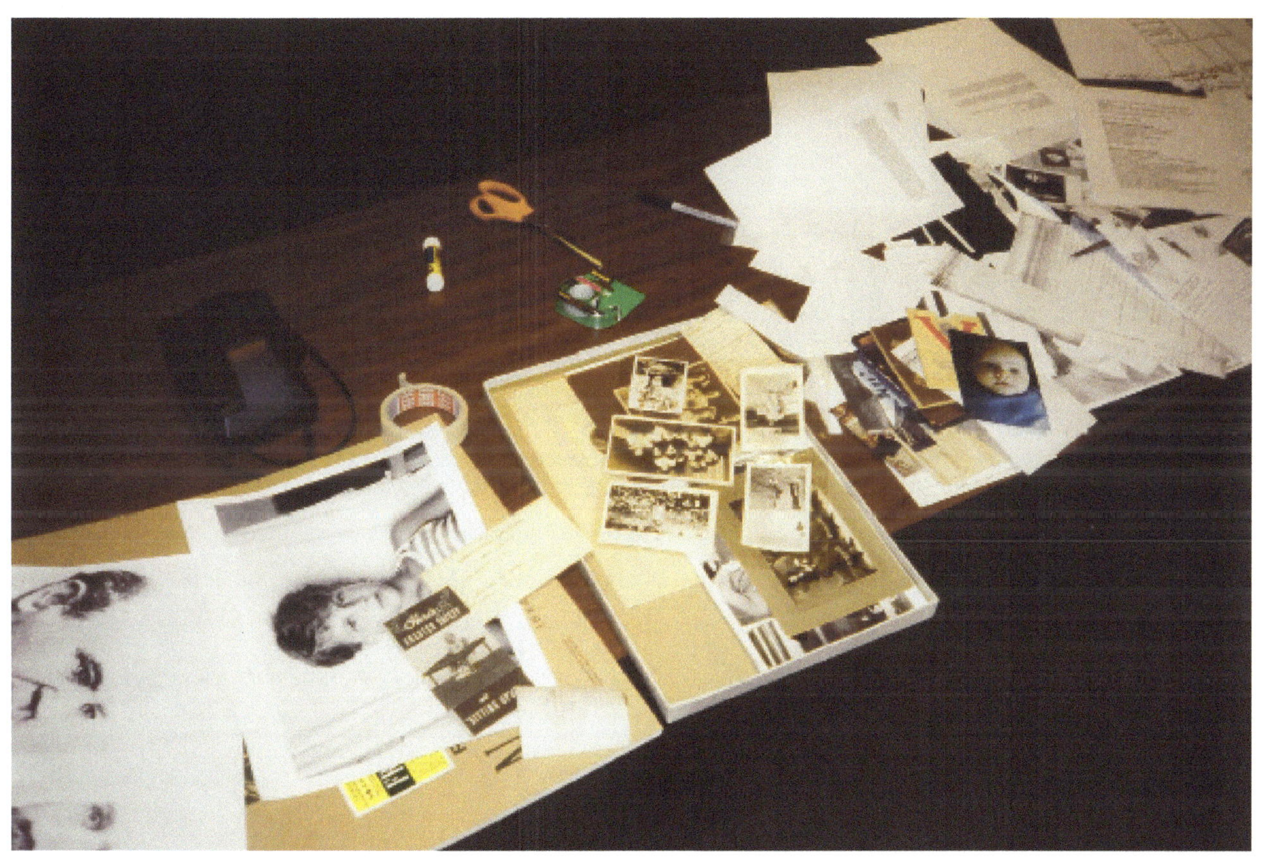

Workbook

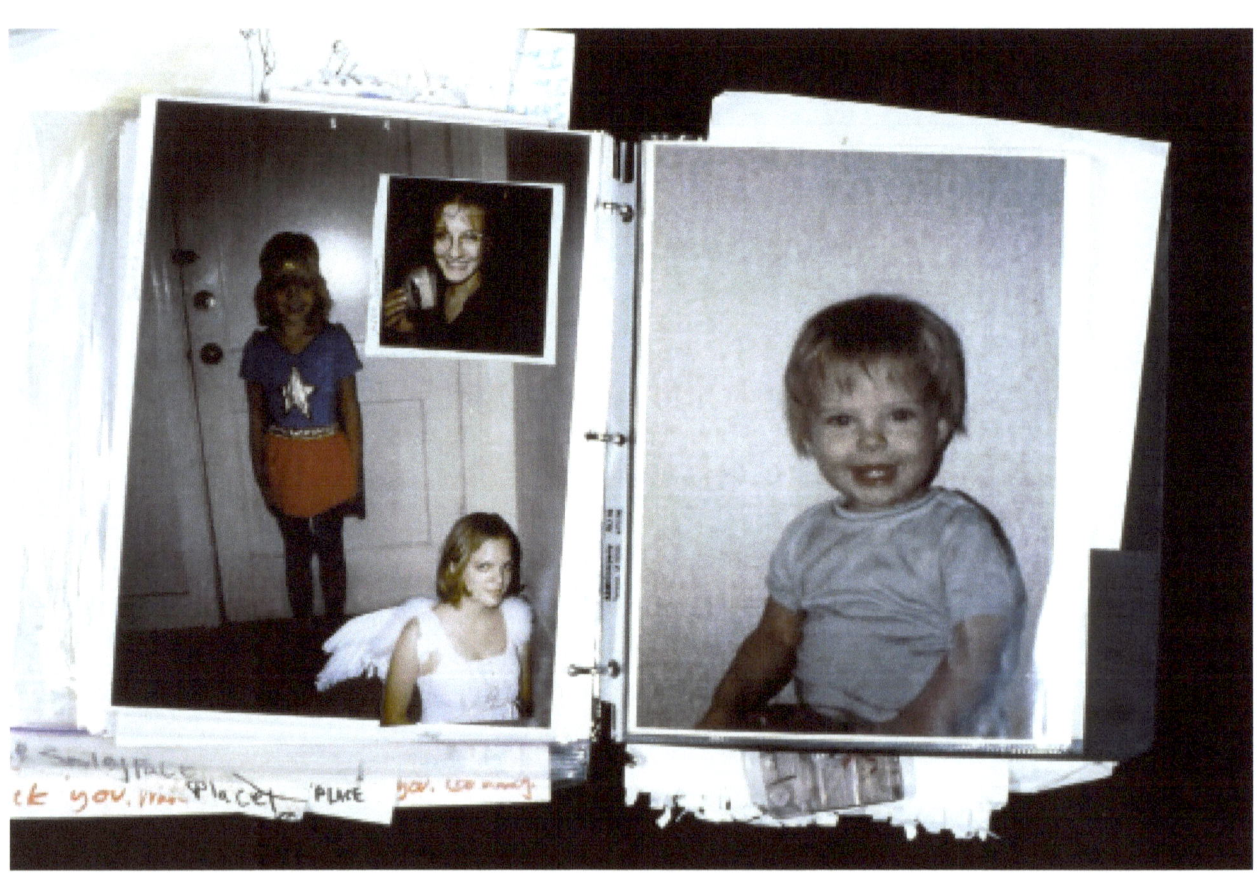

"Everyone is an artist."[1]

Portrait of Self is a process of learning non-linear creative thinking skills, visual organization, visual literacy and research skills. The process can be used to integrate creativity, visual arts and academic learning. The process is meant to add value, new possibilities and alternative methods for learning to a teacher's suitcase of skills.

This basic workbook is a means of gathering resources by which art and academic projects can be enriched. The workbook teaches students to document their daily activities, record memories and learn creative and non-linear thinking processes. The outcome of the workshop can lead to visual arts, theater, creative writing or academic projects. This process can be applied to keeping journals and learning research skills. How the process is put to use is up to the interest and imagination of the facilitator or teacher.

Portrait of Self Archiving Workbook

Portrait of Self (POS) is an arts and educational project to help young people talk about the many influences that create their sense of self. A self-portrait in the most traditional sense is the reproduction of one's own reflection in a mirror. *POS* is an archive of drawings, poetry, writing, photography and other artistic practices. The student creates this archive as a representation of the complexity of life. POS is an investigation of the sources that make up the history of who we are.

This workbook is designed to help challenge habitual ways of approaching issues of social and personal content. POS represents a path for participants to react to and with which to investigate their heritage, families, lifestyles, memories and values using artistic practice and archiving collection methods. It allows students and teachers to investigate difficult personal and social issues such as: race, consumer culture, sexual orientation, gender and religion. The text is not meant to solve social or personal problems, but to provide participants and students with an ongoing means for investigation.

How To Use This Text

I hope that this means of expression will provide artists, teachers and students with an important tool to investigate their own identities and cultures. Students/artists may investigate their sense of self through artistic practice, using writing, dance, photography, poetry, and the visual arts. The students/artist and faculty explore a series of questions, statements and problems leading to the creation of a personal archive. The archive is made up of the participant's responses to the various problems, lists, and questions. The archives are works of art that may be displayed in an exhibition at the end of the project.

There are no correct answers to the questions the text and workshops raise and no specific time period for completion of the archive. The questions and statements are not specific to any one creative discipline, but can be addressed through drawing, writing, acting, discussion, and digital or social media. The choice of artistic practice depends on the love, interest, and passion of the participants. Participants should creatively add to the text with their own questions, lists, and points for discussion. I recommend that the participants respond using a variety of artistic practices; they do not need to be trained in a particular creative discipline [such as drawing] to attempt to use it in responding to the questions. The participant's work does not need to be judged by traditional standards of quality; the questions ask for an honest response. It is important that each participant's work is saved and placed in their individual archive. The total accumulation of documents, drawings, writings, photographs and lists represent the individual's portrait.

Workshop Menu: Directions for Getting Hungry

- Commit yourself to the problem and trust in the situation.

- Don't prejudge or be embarrassed.

- Don't be judgmental.

- Learn to make decisions without rational thought.

- Trust your body.

- Nothing is a mistake; all is an experiment.

- Work leads; it is the people who make that eventually discover.

- There is no possibility of creating work and analyzing it at the same time; they are different processes.

- Concentrate on making work.

- Enjoy yourself and play with a child's intensity.

- Be self-regulating and disciplined; discover your habits and break them.

- Beware! Observation is a form of pre-thinking and prejudice.

Don't be afraid of being dumb!

- Stay hungry.

- Activities do not have to be done in order.

- Add your own problems.

- Do it your way.

- Use different artistic practices.

- Save everything.

Workbook Questions

How we see the world and the people in it is determined by our memory. Seeing is an act of remembering. We see the world through our experiences and prejudices. The following work is meant to break down the habitual way we look at the world and ourselves to provide a fresh start.

Perception is communication between the environment and the mind. Is art the record of an individual processing this communication?

Create a map of your first neighborhood. Mark on the map all the places that you were bad. Continue to mark all the places you were good, and write down all your friends. Who was the first friend you got into a fight with? Keep adding as you work to recall lost memories.

What processes mark the growth of the brain into the mind? How is observation turned into memory? What is the shape and form of memory and thought? How does memory function? How does creative thought occur?

Habit has authority over thinking. Reverse your ideas. What would you not do to a piece of paper? How would you not make a drawing? How would you not express yourself? How would you not make a self-portrait? Make them.

Write about the first time that you "hated" another person. Use a pencil, erase your writing and place the writing in an envelope and seal it. Write the word "hate" on it. Make a list of all the children who were your friends. Circle the one that became your first enemy. Do a portrait of him or her. Write the story about this person and you on the drawing. Change the word hate to love.

Some of our qualities will not change or will only slowly evolve over a lifetime such as: race, age, physical needs, biological makeup, and religion. What symbols represent these qualities for you? Collect the symbols that represent you. Create a self-portrait by making a collage out of the symbols.

Memory is a definition of self. It distorts the process of thinking and seeing. To think and see the world uniquely takes no active effort beyond existence. To express that unique view takes method.

Save the covers of all your notebooks and binders. Do they have drawings on them?

Save all the notes you receive and get back the ones you wrote. Make a special container to hold them. Place them in the container. Are other people allowed to open the container and read the notes? Will this change the way you design your container?

Save all the doodles that you make. Doodles are drawings. Place them in a large brown envelope.

Remember your first house? Go there in your imagination. Walk around in it, draw/write/ record your memory on a sheet of paper, keeping your eyes closed. Do a second drawing with your eyes open. Write the story of your life in this house on the drawing. Use this as the source for a new creative work.

Some of our qualities are in constant change; such as physical appearance, friends, age, status, lifestyle, location, values, marital status, pregnancy, education, employment and income. Make a portrait of your self in constant change.

How will time and life change you? Who will you be when you are 60 years old? Will you live in North Carolina in a trailer park? Write a poem about being old and looking back. Make a portrait of yourself as an old person. Combine the drawing and verses from the poem.

Trust your body. The hand is intelligent. Drawing is the dance of the hand. Make a drawing while you are dancing. Place a sheet of paper on the floor, turn up the music, dance on the paper and save it. It is a document of how you move.

Create yourself as a person with no heritage, no race, no gender, no age, no religion, no sexual orientation, no education, no occupation and no family. Are you happy now? Are you a cartoon character? A super hero? Are you reduced only to your biology?

List all the things you love, all the things you hate and keep the lists going. Which list is the longest? Make a drawing that is a war between the two lists.

Make a drawing about your family, in three ways: draw as you drew when you were 5 years old; then as when you were 12 years old; and finally, as you might draw when you are 30 years old.

Make a drawing with the qualities that make you part of a group, gang, team, family, nationality or race. Use symbols. Where does the self begin to get lost? Where is the line between you as a person and you as a member of the group? Make a drawing of your face and divide it into two sections, making one side you as an individual and one as part of the group.

Get a friend to trace the outline of your body on a large sheet of paper two times. One tracing represents your nationality and ethnic heritage, the other your personal life. Fill in the interior of the tracings with information that represents each category. Do the tracings overlap? What does it mean if they do?

Play creates wonder, or have you forgotten? Learn to play again. Make a work that makes fun of your most serious thoughts.

Turn your life into a board game, draw the board and create the characters. Can you win or lose the game? Are there rules? When does the game end? What do you win? What is the greatest hazard?

Art is play, art is serious, art is play, art is serious, art is play and art is serious. You are play and you are serious. Do a self-portrait showing both qualities.

When was the first time you understood ownership? When was the first time you realized you could not get something because of money, gender, status, race, body size, looks or lifestyle? Make a history of your life based on not getting what you wanted.

Keep a list of all the things you want to buy. Keep adding to it, scratching out the ones you buy or receive.

Make a list of every item you use in a day.

Habits determine how new ideas are received. We constantly reinforce our old habits. New information is always received in terms of old ways of seeing. To be creative we must see the world with new eyes. Photograph yourself as soon as you wake up every day for a week.

What is the earliest piece of clothing that you remember wearing? Make that piece of clothing out of paper and paint. Write a verse describing the room in which you would have worn that garment. Make a list of all the clothes you remember having as a child and keep adding to the list throughout the project.

Create a maze to protect your best friend from harm. What hides in the maze?

Linear thinking leads to a single conclusion and possibility is lost. The rational system leads to continuity, selection, focus, but at the cost of seeing other possibilities.

Collect ephemera from your past: toys, church programs, movie tickets, clothes, hair, combs, and other insignificant objects. Make them important by treating them as a treasure; they quantify your existence. Add them to your archives as photocopies.

We see what memory selects for us. Seeing is individualized by each person's past experience.

Collect all the writings, drawings, objects, lists, ephemera, and place them together in a view box. Think about what should and should not be seen. Arrange the items according to their public and private values.

Work as a collaborative group to create an installation by photocopying documents from your archive. As a group use the photocopies to produce an exhibition/installation. Invite lots of people from your community. How can they participate and add to the exhibition?

These questions are a process to help you investigate your life, and to help you break your habits of seeing and perceiving. Now it is time for you to make up your own questions and use the creative methods you have learned to go forward in continuing to record your life's journey. Good luck.

Works Cited

Introduction

1. Linda Nochlin, *Women, Art, and Power, and Other Essays* (New York: Harper and Row, 1988), 7.

2. Lucy R. Lippard, *The Pink Glass Swan: Selected Feminist Essays on Art* (New York: The New Press, 1995), 7-15.

3. M. Anna Fariello, "Making and Naming: The Lexicon of Studio Craft," in *Extra/Ordinary* ed. Maria Buszek (Durham: Duke University Press, 2011), 24.

4. Suzi Gablik, *The Reenchantment of Art* (New York: Thames and Hudson, 1991), 91-95.

5. "Rirkrit Tiravanija," *culturebase.net*, June 18, 2003, http://www.culturebase.net/artist.php?905.

6. Faye Hirsch, "Rirkrit Tiravanija," *Art in America*, June 7, 2011, accessed January 10, 2013, http://www.artinamericamagazine.com/features/rirkrit-tiravanija/

7. Jerry Saltz, "Conspicuous Consumption," *New York Magazine*, May 7, 2007, www.nymag.com/arts/art/reviews/31511/.

8. Esther Yi, "Is Beck's Sheet Music 'Album' a Cop-Out, Radical Art or Both?" *The Atlantic*, December 11, 2012, http://www.theatlantic.com/entertainment/archive/2012/12/is-becks-sheet-music-album-a-cop-out-radical-art-or-both/266125/.

Thoughts and Experiences in Social Arts Practice

1. Beth Krensky and Seana-Lowe Steffan, *Engaging Classrooms and Communities through Art: A Guide to Designing and Implementing Community-Based Art Education* (Lanham: Altamira Press, 2009), 19.

2. "Fundred Supporting Operation Paydirt," 2010, www.fundred.org.about/.

3. Interview between Adelia Ganson and Mel Chin, January, 2010.

4. Nicolas Bourriaud, *Relational Aesthetics* (Dijon: Les presses du réel, 2002), 13-16.

5. Mary Jane Jacob and Jacquelynn Bass, eds., *Learning Mind: Experience into Art* (Berkeley: University of California Press, 2010), 1-2, 6.

6. John Dewey, *Experience and Education* (New York: Kappa Delta Pi, Touchstone, 1938), 6-20.

7. Ibid., 17-20.

8. Bourriaud, *Relational Aesthetics*, 11.

9. Mary Jane Jacob, "Acknowledgments," in *Places with a Past: New Site Specific Art at Charleston's Spoleto Festival* (New York: Rizzoli, Spoleto Festival, USA, 1991), 10-12.

10. Mary Jane Jacob, "Making History in Charleston," in *Places with a Past*, 13-19.

Criterion for Community Art: Underlying Construct

1. Bourriaud, *Relational Aesthetics*, 13.

2. Harrell Fletcher, Miranda July, *Learning to Love You More* (Munich: Prestel Verlag, 2007), 1.

3. Allan McCollom, "Harrell Fletcher Interviewed by Allan McCollom," *Art 21: Blog*, September 25, 2009, http://blog.art21.org/2009/09/25/harrell-fletcher-interviewed-by-allan-mccollum/

4. Lippard, *The Pink Glass Swan*, 179.

5. Suzanne Lacy, ed., *Mapping the Terrain: New Genre Public Art* (Seattle: Bay Press, 1995), 19.

6. Vivien Green Fryd, "Ending the Silence," in *Doin' it in Public: Feminism and Art at the Woman's Building*, eds. Meg Linton, Sue Maberry, Elizabeth Pulsinelli (Los Angeles: Otis College of Art and Design, 2011), 159-179.

7. Alanna Heiss, "Breaking the Code," in *David Hammons: Rousing the Rubble*, (New York: The Institute for Contemporary Art PS1 Museum, 1991), 28.

8. Ibid., 29.

9. Alain Borer "The Essential Joseph Beuys" in *The Essential Joseph Beuys* ed. Lothar Schirmer (Cambridge: MIT Press, 1997), 18-23.

10. MoMA PS1, "Focus: Joseph Beuys," 2010, http://www.moma.org/visit/calendar/exhibitions/306

11. Doc.Art.com: The Art/Medicine of Eric Avery, M.D., "How to use a Male/Female Condom (toilet paper motif)," 2012, http://www.docart.com/condom/newcondom1.html

12. Ibid.

13. Project Row Houses "about," www.projectrowhouses.org, 2013, http://projectrowhouses.org/about/

14. Ibid.

15. Theatre of the Oppressed, "Techniques," 2004, http://www.theatreoftheoppressed.org/en/index.php?nodeID=74

What Do We Mean by Criterion for Community Art?
1. Ruth Weisberg, "The Syntax of the Print: In Search of an Aesthetic Context," *The Tamarind Papers* (Vol. 9, Fall 1986): 52-60.
2. Lippard, *The Pink Glass Swan*, 118-127 (see chap. 1, n. 2).
3. Krensky and Steffan, *Engaging Classrooms and Communities through Art*, 72 (see chap.1, n.1).

Teaching Fundamentals of Community Arts Practice
1. Kathleen Dean Moore, "If your House is on Fire: Kathleen Dean Moore on the Moral Urgency of Climate Change," *The Sun* 444 (2012): 6-7.
2. Norman L. Kleeblatt, "Greenberg, Rosenberg, and Postwar American Art," in *Action/Abstraction: Pollock, DeKooning, and American Art, 1940-1976*," ed. Norman Kleeblatt (New Haven: Yale University Press, 2008), 135-140.
3. Rackstraw Downes, ed., *Fairfield Porter: Art in its own Terms: Selected Criticism, 1935-1975* (New York: Taplinger Publishing, 1979), 28-29.
4. Kleeblatt, *Action/Abstraction: Pollock, DeKooning*, 145-147.
5. Nochlin, *Women, Art, and Power*, 149 (see chap. 1. n. 1).
6. Ibid., 176.

Roles of the Artists and Community
1. Wendy Ewald, *Secret Games: Collaborative Works with Children 1969-1999*, (New York: Scalo, 1999) 15-18.
2. Ibid.
3. Ian Berry, Julie Ault, Susan Cahan, David Deitcher, et al., *Tim Rollins and the K.O.S.: A History* (Cambridge: MIT Press, 2009), 41-43.
4. Ibid., 14.
5. Interview between Dylan Mortimer and Adelia Ganson, January, 2013.
6. Critical Art Ensemble, "Defense Fund," 2009, http://caedefensefund.org/
7. Ibid.

8. Ibid.
9. Ibid.
10. Jimmy Wang, "In China, a Headless Mao is a Game of Cat and Mouse," *The New York Times*, October, 5, 2009, http://www.nytimes.com/2009/10/06/arts/design/06gao.html?pagewanted=all&_r=0
11. The Library of Congress Prints and Photographs Reading Room: Prints and Photographs Division, "Dorothea Lange's 'Migrant Mother' Photographs in the Farm Securities Administration Collection: An Overview," 2013, http://www.loc.gov/rr/print/list/128_migm.html
12. Jonathan Munar, "Carrie Mae Weems: 'The Kitchen Table Series, '" *Art 21 Blog*, March 18, 2011, 2011/03/18/
13. http://blog.art21.org/2011/03/18/carrie-mae-weems-the-kitchen-table-series/
14. Robert Atkins, *Artspeak* (New York: Abbeville Press, 1990), 84-86.
15. Ibid.
16. Mo Alabi "Ed Hardy: From art to infamy and back again," CNN, September 30, 2013, http://www.cnn.com/2013/09/04/living/fashion-ed-hardy-profile/index.html?iref=allsearch

Teaching Creativity
1. Gilles Deleuze, Felix Guattari, *A Thousand Plateaus*, translation and forward by Brian Massumi (Minneapolis: University of Minnesota Press, 1987), 7.
2. Stanford Encyclopedia of Philosophy, "Gilles Deleuze," September 24, 2012, http://plato.stanford.edu.entries/deleuze
3. Stuart Jeffries, "John Cage: Musicians and Artists on a Legend," *The Guardian*, August 15, 2012, http://www.guardian.co.uk/music/2012/aug/15/john-cage-centenary-tribute
4. Mary Ann Caws, *Surrealism* (New York, London: Phaidon Press, 2004), 14-21.
5. Lucy R. Lippard, *Dadas on Art* (Englewood Cliffs: Prentiss Hall, 1971), 2.
6. Ibid., 139-140.
7. Caws, *Surrealism*, 17-26.
8. Patrick Waldberg, *Surrealism* (New York: Mac-Graw Hill, 1971), 66-75.
9. Poets.org: From the Academy of American Poets,

"Arthur Rimbaud," 2012, http://www.poets.org/
poet.php/prmPID/1268

10. Caws, *Surrealism*, 26.

11. Eric Fischl spoke about his personal creative process at the Nelson-Atkins Museum of Art in Kansas City, Missouri, in April of 2011.

Community Art Assignments

1. Poets.org: From the Academy of American Poets, "Poetic Techniques: Chance Operations," 2012, http://www.poets.org/viewmedia.php/prmMID/5774

2. Warren Bennis and Patricia Ward Biederman, *Organizing Genius: The Secrets of Creative Collaboration*, (New York: Basic Books, 1997), 1-5.

Activities and Projects

1. Harrell Fletcher, Miranda July, *Learning to Love You More*, 150-157 (see chap. 3, n. 2).

2. Edward R. Tufte, *The Visual Display of Quantitative Information*, (Cheshire: Graphics Press, 2001), 13-78.

3. "Kansas City Jewish Museum of Contemporary Art," 2013, http://www.kcjmca.org/home/

4. Sandra Hayes, Lyle Yorks, eds., "Arts and Societal Learning: Transforming Communities Socially, Politically and Culturally," *New Directions for Adult and Continuing Education* 116 (Winter, 2007): 91.

Portrait of Self workbook

1. Götz Adriani, Winfried Konnertz, and Karin Thomas, *Joseph Beuys: Life and Works*, trans. Patricia Lech, (New York: Barron's Educational Series, 1979), 255.

www.ingramcontent.com/pod-product-compliance
Lightning Source LLC
Chambersburg PA
CBHW042148030726
47599CB00004B/660